D1191529

America's Failure in Vietnam

Titles in the History's Great Defeats series include:

The Aztecs: End of a Civilization
The British Empire: The End of Colonialism
The Cold War: Collapse of Communism
The Crusades: Failed Holy Wars
The French Revolution: The Fall of the Monarchy
The Indian Wars: From Frontier to Reservation
The Napoleonic Wars: Defeat of the Grand Army
The Third Reich: Demise of the Nazi Dream

America's Failure in Vietnam

by Richard Brownell

Valley Cottage Library
110 Route 303
Valley Cottage, NY 10989

LUCENT BOOKS

An imprint of Thomson Gale, a part of The Thomson Corporation

THOMSON

™

GALE

Detroit • New York • San Francisco • San Diego • New Haven, Conn.
Waterville, Maine • London • Munich

The Vietnam Service Medal was awarded to all members of the armed forces who served in Vietnam and contiguous waters and airspace, or who served in Thailand, Laos, or Cambodia in direct support of operations in Vietnam , between July 1965 and March 1973.

© 2005 Thomson Gale, a part of The Thomson Corporation.

Thomson and Star Logo are trademarks and Gale and Lucent Books are registered trademarks used herein under license.

For more information, contact
Lucent Books
27500 Drake Rd.
Farmington Hills, MI 48331-3535
Or you can visit our Internet site at http://www.gale.com

LIBRARY OF CONGRESS CATALOGING-IN-PUBLICATION DATA

Brownell, Richard. (1972–)
  America's failure in Vietnam / by Richard Brownell.
    p. cm. — (History's great defeats)
  Includes bibliographical references and index.
  ISBN 1-59018-695-8 (hardcover : alk. paper)
  1. Vietnamese Conflict, 1961–1975—United States. 2. United States—History—1945– I. Title.
II. Series.
DS558.B78 2005
959.704'3373--dc22
                                                              2004028891

Printed in the United States of America

Table of Contents

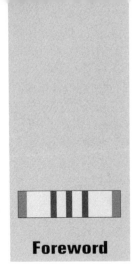

Foreword

HISTORY IS FILLED with tales of dramatic encounters that sealed the fates of empires or civilizations, changing them or causing them to disappear forever. One of the best known events began in 334 B.C., when Alexander, king of Macedonia, led his small but formidable Greek army into Asia. In the short span of only ten years, he brought Persia, the largest empire the world had yet seen, to its knees, earning him the nickname forever after associated with his name—"the Great." The demise of Persia, which at its height stretched from the shores of the Mediterranean Sea in the west to the borders of India in the east, was one of history's most stunning defeats. It occurred primarily because of some fatal flaws in the Persian military system, disadvantages the Greeks had exploited before, though never as spectacularly as they did under Alexander.

First, though the Persians had managed to conquer many peoples and bring huge territories under their control, they had failed to create an individual fighting man who could compare with the Greek hoplite. A heavily armored infantry soldier, the hoplite fought in a highly effective and lethal battlefield formation—the phalanx. Possessed of better armor, weapons, and training than the Persians, Alexander's soldiers repeatedly crushed their Persian opponents. Second, the Persians for the most part lacked generals of the caliber of their Greek counterparts. And when Alexander invaded, Persia had the added and decisive disadvantage of facing one of the greatest generals of all time. When the Persians were defeated, their great empire was lost forever.

Other world powers and civilizations have fallen in a like manner. They have succumbed to some combination of inherent fatal flaws or

6

disadvantages, to political and/or military mistakes, and even to the personal failings of their leaders.

Another of history's great defeats was the sad demise of the North American Indian tribes at the hands of encroaching European civilization from the sixteenth to nineteenth centuries. In this case, all of the tribes suffered from the same crippling disadvantages. Among the worst, they lacked the great numbers, the unity, and the advanced industrial and military hardware possessed by the Europeans. Still another example, one closer to our own time, was the resounding defeat of Nazi Germany by the Allies in 1945, which brought World War II, the most disastrous conflict in history, to a close. Nazi Germany collapsed for many reasons. But one of the most telling was that its leader, Adolf Hitler, sorely underestimated the material resources and human resolve of the Allies, especially the United States. In the end, Germany was in a very real sense submerged by a massive and seemingly relentless tidal wave of Allied bombs, tanks, ships, and soldiers.

Seen in retrospect, a good many of the fatal flaws, drawbacks, and mistakes that caused these and other great defeats from the pages of history seem obvious. It is only natural to wonder why, in each case, the losers did not realize their limitations and/or errors sooner and attempt to avert disaster. But closer examination of the events, social and political trends, and leading personalities involved usually reveals that complex factors were at play. Arrogance, fear, ignorance, stubbornness, innocence, and other attitudes held by nations, peoples, and individuals often colored and shaped their reactions, goals, and strategies. And it is both fascinating and instructive to reconstruct how such attitudes, as well as the fatal flaws and mistakes themselves, contributed to the losers' ultimate demise.

Each volume in Lucent Books' *History's Great Defeats* series is designed to provide the reader with diverse learning tools for exploring the topic at hand. Each well-informed, clearly written text is supported and enlivened by substantial quotes by the actual people involved, as well as by later historians and other experts; and these primary and secondary sources are carefully documented. Each volume also supplies the reader with an extensive Works Consulted list, guiding him or her to further research on the topic. These and other research tools, including glossaries and time lines, afford the reader a thorough understanding of how and why one of history's most decisive defeats occurred and how these events shaped our world.

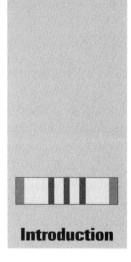

America Inherits
Introduction a Civil War

If they force us into war, we will fight. The struggle will be atrocious, but the Vietnamese people will suffer anything rather than renounce their freedom.

—Ho Chi Minh

IN THE YEARS following World War II the United States found itself engaged in the Cold War—a worldwide struggle to contain the spread of communism. The Soviet Union, an ally in the battle to defeat the Germans and the Japanese, quickly became America's principal nemesis as it aggressively pushed to spread its empire beyond its vast borders. By 1949, through political subterfuge, material support of Communist insurgents, and direct military intervention, the Soviets had brought much of Eastern Europe under its control, and were looking to expand in the East. The fall of China to the Communist forces of Mao Zedong that same year alarmed American policy makers, who lobbied for a greater U.S. presence in Asia, where the French were embroiled in a war with Communist insurgents in their colony of Vietnam.

Vietnam: A History of Strife
The country of Vietnam was part of a larger French colonial holding known as Indochina, which also included modern-day Cambodia and Laos. The battle to break France's hold on Vietnam was the latest in the centuries-long Vietnamese struggle to define their own destiny. For hundreds of years before the arrival of the French, Vietnam often found

8

itself at war with imperial China, which attempted several times to sub-due the nation for its own interests. There were also internal power struggles between the northern and southern regions of Vietnam, as competing families vied for control.

This rampant turmoil, together with the country's plentiful re-sources of spice, rubber, and rice, made Vietnam ripe for colonial ex-ploitation. After the first Catholic missionaries entered the country in the early 1600s, French influence in the region steadily expanded over the following two centuries, culminating in the military takeover of the southern city of Saigon in 1861. The French colonial power deconstructed the old Confucian order in favor of a Catholic hierar-chy, adapted and replaced the traditional written Vietnamese language with a Roman version, and enforced French legal and educational stan-dards on the population.

These massive changes led to further unrest among the Vietnamese, and the French routinely faced resistance. Naval commander Admi-ral Louis-Adolphe Bonard remarked in 1862, "We have had enormous

French soldiers engage Vietnamese rebels in battle in the 1880s. Throughout the late 1800s, rebel bands throughout Vietnam routinely harried French colonial troops.

difficulties in enforcing our authority. . . . Rebel bands disturb the country everywhere. They appear from nowhere in large numbers, destroy everything and then disappear into nowhere."[1] This unrest continued with little effect for decades until the various anticolonial groups became a united front.

The French Bail Out

In 1941, after thirty years abroad, Ho Chi Minh, a committed Communist revolutionary, returned to his native land of Vietnam intent on freeing his people from the French and establishing a Communist government. Through coercion and force Ho consolidated under his control, the scattered independence movements and with the help of his colleagues Pham Van Dong and Vo Nguyen Giap, formed the Vietminh.

During World War II the Vietminh worked with American forces then battling the Japanese domination of Asia, and Ho had hoped the United States would in turn support the removal of the French. President Franklin D. Roosevelt had once noted, "France has milked [Vietnam] for one hundred years. The people of Indochina are entitled to something better than that."[2] Roosevelt's view of an independent Vietnam, however, was a minority one and the idea died with him on April 12, 1945.

On September 2, 1945, the day that Japan formally surrendered to the Allies, Ho publicly declared Vietnam an independent nation with himself as president, quoting from the American Declaration of Independence in his speech. He sought American recognition of the new nation but was rebuked because of his Communist leanings. The French, whose hold on Vietnam had been substantially weakened during World War II, returned with expectations of restoring their rule. Ho's Vietminh clashed with France for control of the country in a bitter war that slowly bled dry France's military capability and will to fight.

As their hold on Vietnam became more precarious, France turned to the United States for assistance. In 1950 President Harry S. Truman authorized $15 million in military aid, noting, "We could not deny military aid to a victim of Communist aggression in Asia unless we wanted other small nations to swing into the Soviet camp."[3] The United States provided $3 billion in material aid over the next four years, amounting to 80 percent of the total French war expense, but it made little dif-

Ho Chi Minh

Born Nguyen Sinh Cung in 1890, the man who would become known to the world as Ho Chi Minh (He Who Enlightens) spent much of his time before World War II traveling the world and becoming familiar with socialist ideology and communism. Ho brought what he learned back to his native land of Vietnam in order to free his people from the French colonial occupation.

During World War II Ho's Vietminh forces worked with American military personnel toward the common goal of defeating the Japanese presence in Southeast Asia. Ho was skeptical, however, of America's willingness to help Vietnam achieve full independence from France, as explained in William J. Duiker's biography, *Ho Chi Minh:*

> Ho viewed the United States as a crucial but enigmatic factor in his country's struggle for national independence. . . . President [Franklin] Roosevelt had emerged during the Pacific War as one of the most powerful and vocal spokesmen for the liberation of the oppressed peoples of Asia . . . and Ho apparently held out the possibility that Roosevelt's policies would continue to shape U.S. attitudes after the close of the war.
>
> On the other hand, if tensions rose between the [United States] and the USSR, Washington might decide to make concessions to Paris in order to enlist the French in an effort to prevent the spread of communism.

A Communist revolutionary, Ho Chi Minh is credited with driving the French out of Vietnam.

ference. Lack of a concerted strategy for defeating the Vietminh and an inability to gather local support for their cause led to the resounding defeat of the French at Dien Bien Phu on May 7, 1954, and the subsequent end of France's involvement in Vietnam.

After the French began pulling out of Indochina, representatives from the United States, Britain, France, Laos, Cambodia, the Soviet Union, China, and Vietnam met to discuss the future of Vietnam. The result of this meeting was the Geneva Accord, which divided Vietnam at the seventeenth parallel into two states, with Ho's Vietminh ruling the North, and the non-Communist emperor Bao Dai ruling the South. Another principal point of the agreement called for general elections in July 1956 to reunify the country.

The United States and South Vietnam feared that any such election would lead to South Vietnam falling under the Communist domination of North Vietnam, and they rejected the Geneva Accord. Despite the U.S. and South Vietnamese rejection of the Geneva Accord, Ho remained committed to uniting the nation under communism by any means necessary.

America's Reluctant Involvement

When the French evacuated Vietnam, America was the only Western power left that would support the fledgling non-Communist nation in the South. U.S. president Dwight D. Eisenhower remained concerned

 **The Domino Theory**

The United States was forced to adapt its foreign policy to defend against Soviet expansion after World War II. The rapid spread of communism demonstrated a need to answer the USSR's aggressive actions anywhere in the world, particularly in Southeast Asia. The reasoning behind this new policy lay in the "domino theory," first publicly defined by President Dwight D. Eisenhower in 1954, and explained in James R. Arnold's *The First Domino: Eisenhower, the Military, and America's Intervention in Vietnam:*

> [A] reporter asked the President to explain what Indochina meant to the free world. In his response, Eisenhower . . . said: "Finally, you have broader considerations that might follow what you would call the 'falling domino' principle. You have a row of dominoes set up, you knock over the first one, and what will happen to the last one is the certainty that it will go over very quickly." He then listed the dominoes in order: Indochina, Burma, Thailand, Malaysia, Indonesia. One after another, the shock wave of their fall would extend all the way to Japan, Formosa, the Philippines, Australia, and New Zealand. He concluded: "The possible consequences of the loss are just incalculable."

about containing the spread of communism in Asia, but he was reluctant to engage significant American resources to the endeavor. The United States had secured a cease-fire to end the Korean War in 1953, which had cost over thirty-five thousand American lives and ended in a stalemate. The nation was not willing to pay such a high price again for so little gain.

Ho quietly sent thousands of Vietminh infiltrators into South Vietnam between 1955 and 1960, while America continued to supply the country with military and civilian advisers and more than $2 billion in aid. The United States pinned its hopes for a stable government on Ngo Dinh Diem, South Vietnam's prime minister and, later, president. Diem's rule did not reflect the concerns of the people of South Vietnam, and his government, populated by family members and political cronies, was rampantly corrupt. Yet, as Secretary of State John Foster Dulles noted in 1954, in order to prevent a Communist takeover of the country, "we have no choice but [to] continue our aid [to] Vietnam and support of Diem."[4]

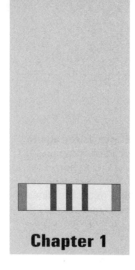

South Vietnam: An Uncertain Ally

Chapter 1

[T]here must be a heartfelt cause to which the legitimate government is pledged, a cause which makes a stronger appeal to the people than the Communist cause.

—General Edward Lansdale

IN PLANNING STRATEGY for combating communism in Southeast Asia, American policy makers operated from the assumption that the government of South Vietnam was strong enough to defend itself and defeat the Communist insurgence from the North with a modicum of U.S. military and economic aid. This belief proved false because South Vietnam's leaders were frequently corrupt and generally poor administrators, and they were often out of touch with the needs of the South Vietnamese people. Their harsh and violent methods of maintaining order created an atmosphere of distrust among the populace that the Vietcong, or VC, as the North Vietnamese insurgents were known, used to their own advantage. Arthur M. Schlesinger Jr., adviser to President John F. Kennedy and author of *A Thousand Days: John F. Kennedy in the White House,* noted that "the Vietcong could never be defeated unless the Saigon regime could enlist the support of the peasants."[5]

Despite the severe shortcomings of the rulers in Saigon, America continued to pledge its support to the fractured South Vietnamese government, thereby committing one of the first grievous mistakes in its involvement in Vietnam. Since the U.S. government felt that it could not walk away from its commitment without risking a Communist takeover of South Vietnam, it was forced to take an ever larger role in the war as the political situation in South Vietnam continued to disintegrate.

The Leadership Vacuum

Problems with the South Vietnamese government developed almost from the beginning. Diem seized power from the complacent emperor Bao Dai in a rigged election on October 23, 1955, and assumed the presidency. James William Gibson notes in *The Perfect War: Technowar in Vietnam,* "In Saigon, [Diem] received more votes than registered voters—98%; of 605,025 votes cast when there were approximately 450,000 registered voters."[6] Diem was publicly praised by Eisenhower as the Miracle Man of Asia. Privately, the U.S. government was only modestly confident in Diem's abilities to run the country.

As a leader, Diem placed a higher value on personal loyalty than administrative ability. He filled top government and army positions with family members and political cronies, many of whom proved incompetent for the tasks assigned to them. Those who did show initiative and intelligence generally disagreed with Diem's decisions. Intolerant of dissent, Diem often had these men ousted, sometimes jailed, or even executed.

U.S. president Dwight D. Eisenhower (left) meets with South Vietnamese president Ngo Dinh Diem (center) in 1957. Eisenhower had little confidence in Diem's ability to govern Vietnam.

Diem openly favored those in the government and the country at large who shared his religious sentiments and appointed civil and military administrators based on their Catholic faith. His Catholic background did not endear him to the largely Buddhist population, and he was often intolerant of their religious institutions and practices. Despite these shortcomings Kennedy was willing to continue supporting Diem because there had been noticeable improvement, as Schlesinger notes in *A Thousand Days:* "He had subdued the religious sects, cleaned up Saigon, and with American aid, brought about a measure of economic growth and social improvement. Living standards, indeed, had risen faster in South than in North Vietnam."[7]

Problems developed, however, as the VC insurgency gained momentum. The South Vietnamese military was largely ineffective due to a lack of skilled commanders and rampant corruption and could not keep the Communists from infiltrating the rural areas. In January 1963 South Vietnamese forces were defeated by a much smaller VC force at Ap Bac. The scope of this defeat was downplayed by U.S. Army chief of staff Earle Wheeler to prevent questioning by skeptics of American support. However, the social problems in Diem's regime could not be minimized.

In May Buddhists rioted after being denied the right to properly celebrate the Buddha's birthday. Being unfamiliar with the concepts of democracy and compromise, Diem relied on force to quell the demonstrations, and several Buddhists were killed by South Vietnamese police, led by Diem's brother Ngo Dinh Nhu. The United States was angered by this event and threatened to remove aid if Diem did not remove corrupt officials and enact solid national reforms.

Diem did not make any real attempts at reform, but the Americans did not make good on threats to pull support either. It was obvious to policy makers in Washington that if the aid stopped, Diem's regime would collapse and chaos would ensue. As a result, neither the South Vietnamese government nor the American government made any changes.

The North Vietnamese capitalized on the social unrest by providing further aid to the VC in the South. "[Diem] is unpopular, and the more unpopular he is, the more American aid he will need to remain in power," noted North Vietnam prime minister Pham Van Dong. "And the more American aid he gets, the more of an American puppet he'll look, and the less likely he is to regain popularity."[8]

The Suicide of Thich Quang Duc

On May 8, during the celebration of the 2,527th birthday of the Buddha in Hue, nine people were killed when government forces led by President Ngo Dinh Diem violently enforced a decree that prevented the Buddhists from flying their flag. What happened next is illustrated in Lloyd C. Gardner's *Pay Any Price: Lyndon Johnson and the Wars for Vietnam:*

> On the morning of June 11, foreign reporters were alerted by telephone to be present at a busy intersection in the heart of Saigon. There . . . an elderly Buddhist monk named Thich Quang Duc . . . seated himself in the lotus position while his companions poured a can of gasoline over him.

Quang Duc then lit himself on fire, remaining in a position of prayer while the flames consumed him. He fell over dead moments later.

> Pedestrians fell to the ground, prostrating themselves in reverence; trucks and automobiles stopped, snarling traffic. Buddhist monks took advantage of the situation to hand reporters copies of the biography of the suicide. The document included his last words, a "respectful" plea to Diem to show "charity and compassion" to all religions. More immolations followed Quang Duc's suicide. After this episode, many of Diem's supporters in the United States realized that his position was no longer tenable.

On June 11, 1963, Buddhist monk Thich Quang Duc lights himself on fire to protest South Vietnam's repressive religious policies.

In October American ambassador to South Vietnam Henry Cabot Lodge informed Kennedy that members of the South Vietnamese army, known as the Army of the Republic of Vietnam (ARVN), planned to remove Diem from power. Kennedy approved of the coup, since there would be no direct U.S. involvement, but the Joint Chiefs of Staff and members of Kennedy's administration did not support the coup because they believed that it would weaken the U.S. position in the country.

Nevertheless, on November 2, 1963, Diem was overthrown by General Duong Van Minh and was murdered along with his brother Nhu. Kennedy had hoped for a bloodless transfer of power and was shocked when he heard the news of Diem's death. Many in Saigon, however, were overjoyed at the downfall of Diem's regime. Minh, however, proved to be no improvement. H.R. McMaster notes in *Dereliction of Duty: Lyndon Johnson, Robert McNamara, the Joint Chiefs of Staff and the Lies That Led to the Vietnam War,* that the Joint Chiefs remarked that "other than being weak, dumb, and lazy, Minh was well qualified for the South Vietnamese presidency."[9]

Premier Nguyen Cao Ky (on podium, right) salutes an officer as President Nguyen Van Thieu (on podium, center) looks on. Thieu and Ky were part of a rapid succession of military leaders in South Vietnam.

After Minh, there was a rapid succession of military rulers in South Vietnam, with each coup bringing more instability to the country and greater opportunities for the North Vietnamese to instill chaos. Minh was replaced after only two months when it was discovered that he was looking to negotiate a settlement with the Communist National Liberation Front, the principal supporters of the VC in the South. His successors, General Nguyen Khanh and, later, army general Nguyen Van Thieu and the flamboyant air force general Nguyen Cao Ky, proved no more capable in their leadership abilities.

Many American policy makers were disgusted by the poor quality of leadership in the South Vietnamese government. William Bundy, an adviser to President Lyndon Johnson, called Thieu and Ky "the bottom of the barrel, absolutely the bottom of the barrel."[10] General Maxwell Taylor, who succeeded Lodge as ambassador, scolded the generals for their rampant power shifts, but his actions were interpreted by the men as being that of a colonial administrator. Undersecretary of State George Ball summed up the problem with South Vietnam's leadership in a memo to Johnson on June 28, 1965: "South Vietnam is a country with an army and no government. Even if we were to commit five hundred thousand men to South Vietnam, we would still lose."[11]

The leadership vacuum in Saigon settled after September 1967, when elections were held at Johnson's behest. Thieu was elected president and remained in power until South Vietnam fell to the Communists in 1975. His continuous administrative presence offered a certain degree of stability, but he lacked solid leadership skills. A colleague noted, "He failed to grasp what was happening to him in his own country. . . . Thieu could not summon the stature to look beyond himself."[12]

A Dissatisfied Nation

Many South Vietnamese had given up on their government long before Thieu was elected president. The discontent that the population felt with Diem's regime continued with the string of military leaders who followed, none of whom brought any significant improvement to the nation.

Diem never lived up to his promise of meaningful land reform, and the peasants in the rural areas continued to be exploited by wealthy landowners, many of whom were Catholic refugees who fled from the North. These landlords controlled half the cultivated land in the country and demanded up to one-third of farmers' yearly output in rent. Their political influence prevented any tangible reform legislation from being crafted. Furthermore, whenever the military recovered territory from the VC and returned it to the landlords, they would assist in collecting back rent from the peasants.

The VC recognized the burden that the rural population faced and focused their revolutionary efforts on the peasants. It was in this group that the insurgents found recruits, information, and supplies. In order to prevent the VC from gaining any significant support from the peasants, the South Vietnamese government began a rural pacification program. The purpose of this program was to isolate the rural population from the insurgents, consequently denying the Vietcong a source of recruitment and support.

The program consisted of forcibly relocating the rural population to strategic hamlets, which were basically fortified villages that peasants were often ordered to build themselves. The Americans did not understand, and the South Vietnamese government did not care, about the close attachment the peasants held to the land they were taken away from. As a result, the relocation caused bitter resentment among peasants whose religious beliefs held that they should live close to where their ancestors were buried.

The strategic hamlet program became increasingly corrupt over time. Since the creation of new hamlets demonstrated progress in the pacification effort to U.S policy makers, South Vietnamese officials often falsified reports to justify continued American aid. Money for construction went into the pockets of South Vietnamese officers, and hamlets were subdivided in order to boost the number of fortified villages that existed on paper. One American adviser observed, "If you stand still long enough down here, they'll throw a piece of barbed wire around you and call you a strategic hamlet."[13]

When such pacification efforts did not work, American planes bombed suspected Vietcong positions in the South, using traditional explosives, toxic defoliants like Agent Orange to remove the greenery of the jungle, and napalm, a gasoline-based jelly that stuck to and burned whatever and whomever it touched.

The incessant bombing on friendly territory led to the destruction of arable lands and created a massive refugee problem, with more than 4 million rural citizens relocating to the cities. People were herded

The Strategic Hamlet Program

Concerned with the influence the Vietcong were having on the peasants in rural areas, the South Vietnamese government implemented the strategic hamlet program in February 1962. A series of fortified villages were built across the South where rural Vietnamese were relocated away from the reach of the Vietcong.

Dougles Pike explains the varying views of this program in *Vietcong: The Organization and Techniques of the National Liberation Front of South Vietnam:*

> To the Diem government the strategic hamlet was an intensified population-control measure to enable it to tighten its hold on rural Vietnamese by grouping them physically into manageable units, separated from guerilla bands. To the Americans the strategic hamlet was . . . an opportunity for meaningful systematic social welfare work or "winning the hearts of the people" . . . the strategic hamlet was to become a safe island in the midst of a sea of insecurity. . . .

> There was little in the strategic hamlet program for the rural Vietnamese. Not only was he expected to contribute much but he was deprived of his freedom of movement . . . he was in many cases deprived of his land without adequate compensation, and the quarters given him . . . were not as adequate as those he had left.

The conditions that the rural South Vietnamese were forced to live under in these hamlets resembled that of a concentration camp and eventually drove many of them into the arms of the Vietcong, making the strategic hamlet program an abject failure.

---

into makeshift camps that were poorly constructed and unsanitary. Many caught dysentery or malaria. With no jobs to be had, many others became beggars, prostitutes, pickpockets, or muggers.

Despite this sordid state of affairs, American military advisers who supported the pacification program welcomed the influx of peasants into the cities, believing it would deny the North Vietnamese the source of support they were counting on. What the advisers failed to realize was that the appalling conditions that were being created in the cities were driving many people into the arms of the Vietcong. Their inability to understand this was part of a wider cultural misunderstanding that hampered America's involvement in Southeast Asia.

The Cultural Rift

The United States's widespread presence in Vietnam created a vast American subculture within Southeast Asia that was viewed increasingly with resentment by the native population. In 1969, at the height of America's involvement in Vietnam, more than 540,000 troops were in the country. Hundreds of thousands more also traveled through the South in various supporting military and civilian administrative roles, bringing with them Western values and styles of dress that influenced Vietnamese youth. Crime, prostitution, gambling, and drunkenness—all sad by-products of the American military presence—also became more prevalent. Many older Vietnamese were reminded of the French colonial occupation, when Western white people with no knowledge or respect for their culture ruled over their lives.

The Americans, like the French, did not understand the Vietnamese language, nor did they have a grasp of the intricacies of Vietnamese culture. The strong sense of community that the Vietnamese held often led them to reject outsiders, and they became particularly upset

A performer entertains American troops in Vietnam in 1967. By 1969 more than 540,000 U.S. troops were stationed in Vietnam.

about the micro-management of their administrative affairs by U.S. officials. They believed that U.S. policy makers ten thousand miles away
were looking to Westernize their lifestyle.

The growing resentment toward American meddling was not picked
up in Washington, or, if it was, it was ignored. Secretary of State Dean
Rusk noted, "Somehow we must change the pace at which these people move, and I suspect that this can only be done with a pervasive
intrusion of Americans into their affairs."[14]

The Americanization of the War

The less capable the South Vietnamese government proved itself in
handling the affairs of the country, the more involved America became
in Southeast Asia. Townsend Hoopes, undersecretary of the air force
from 1967 to 1969, notes this in his book *The Limits of Intervention*.
"Finding the [South Vietnamese government] incapable of defending
its territory, convinced of the domino theory, and fearing for our own
prestige and security, we had taken over the military side of the struggle."[15]

America's stepped-up involvement began in 1961, when Kennedy
began sending large numbers of military advisers to train the ARVN
in using the vast amounts of American military equipment that was being shipped to Southeast Asia. Like Eisenhower before him, Kennedy
was reticent to engage American resources in Vietnam, but he did not
want to appear soft on communism, particularly after the aborted Bay
of Pigs invasion in Cuba failed to oust Fidel Castro's Communist regime
in April. During the Cold War being labeled as soft on communism
was a political charge leveled by conservatives that could severely
weaken any American leader. Avoiding this stigma affected on some
level many of the decisions that Kennedy, and later Johnson, made con-
cerning Vietnam.

On November 1, 1961, Taylor, then military adviser to the president, recommended sending troops to Vietnam. He warned Kennedy,
however, that "if the first contingent is not enough to accomplish the
necessary results, it will be difficult to resist the pressure to reinforce."[16]

Taylor's words proved true. Instruction teams that were sent to
assist the ARVN led to combat support and air reconnaissance personnel, and later pilots, mechanics, and technicians. The support Americans were providing increasingly put them in harm's way, and they

The National
Liberation Front

The National Liberation Front (NLF) was organized by the North Vietnamese Communists to marshal the resources of the rural population in South Vietnam to overthrow the government there. As Douglas Pike explains in *Vietcong: The Organization and Techniques of the National Liberation Front of South Vietnam,* the NLF proved to be remarkably successful while managing to elude U.S. and South Vietnamese forces.

The NLF did not grow from a small to a large organization; the NLF created on paper a nationwide network of village associations and then proceeded to turn this paper structure into reality. For this reason NLF references to obviously nonexistent organizations in the 1960–1962 period led Vietnamese and Americans in Vietnam to believe that the NLF was only a phantom edifice created for propaganda purposes.

Four years of tireless effort, from 1959 through 1962, converted the NLF organizational structure from a loose, disparate collection of dissident groups, often with nothing more in common than hostility for the Diem government, into a tightly knit movement able to demonstrate a coordinated efficiency rare in a developing nation. That this machine was assembled secretively, by night, in the remote back country makes it even more impressive . . . [and] its nocturnal, clandestine nature helped to ensure its success.

were forced to defend themselves.

At a press conference in February 1962 Kennedy flatly denied that Americans were involved in combat, but columnist James Reston wrote a different take on the situation. "The United States is now involved in an undeclared war in South Vietnam. This is well known to the Russians, the Chinese Communists and everyone else concerned except the American people."[17]

The American effort to support the ARVN was made more difficult by the corruption that existed in South Vietnamese civil and military institutions. Officers were open to bribes by soldiers who sought assignments away from combat. Deserters were rarely reported so that their commanders could continue to receive their combat pay. Other officers deliberately avoided engaging known VC positions, and their tactics were cynically referred to as "search and avoid" by their American counterparts. General apathy came over many in the South Vietnamese military who believed that the Americans would simply take up the fight if ARVN units chose not to, removing the sense of urgency in the struggle against the VC.

Despite these problems Kennedy clung to the belief that the South Vietnamese would be able to continue the fight against the Communists without major American combat support. In a September 3, 1963, television interview, he stated, "In the final analysis, it is their war. They are the ones who have to win it or lose it. We can help them, we can give them equipment, we can send our men over there as advisers, but they have to win it."[18] After Kennedy's assassination on November 22, 1963, Johnson would oversee a much larger troop buildup than Kennedy, or the country, had ever envisioned.

General William Westmoreland, the commander of U.S. forces in Vietnam, told Johnson in the spring of 1965 that only a substantial U.S. military presence would prevent the collapse of South Vietnam's government. The escalation that followed was epic in scale, with large numbers of troops, as well as army engineers and private contractors, descending on South Vietnam. Stanley Karnow notes the scope of the buildup in *Vietnam: A History,*

> Their giant tractors and bulldozers and cranes carved out roads and put up bridges. . . . In the Mekong Delta they dredged the river to create a six-hundred-acre island. . . . They constructed hundreds of helicopter pads and scores of airfields, including huge jet strips at Da Nang and Bienhoa. . . . Almost overnight, they built six new deep-draft harbors, among them a gigantic complex at Cam Ranh Bay, which they completed at breakneck speed by towing prefabricated floating piers across the Pacific.[19]

The troop buildup matched the construction marathon, with levels going from 23,000 in 1964 to 184,000 in 1965. In 1969, after nearly a decade of direct involvement, America had 540,000 soldiers fighting in Vietnam. This number does not reflect the additional air force personnel in Thailand, the Philippines, and Guam, or the naval personnel off the coast at Yankee Station, the name given to the permanent navy presence in the South China Sea during the war. Close to forty percent of the U.S. Army's combat-ready divisions were involved in Vietnam at America's peak of commitment. Nearly half of the U.S.

Children wave as U.S. Marines arrive in Da Nang in 1965. In that year, President Johnson began deploying large numbers of troops to South Vietnam.

Marine Corps, one-third of the navy, and close to half of all the air force fighter bombers and B-52 bombers were also engaged in Southeast Asia.

This heightened military commitment was a result in part of America's continued reliance on a string of unstable leaders in South Vietnam to stop the spread of communism. Unfortunately, as the United States moved further into a war it had not intended to fight, many political and military figures misinterpreted the true nature of the enemy, believing that America could defeat the Vietcong and the North Vietnamese Army (NVA) much as it had opponents in previous wars. This lack of judgment would force the United States to pay a heavier price than the government, the military, or the American public ever expected.

A New
Chapter 2 Kind of War

In Vietnam, by the nature of the fighting, there was never a front line, only a confused ebb and flow of separate and seemingly unrelated small actions.

—General Maxwell Taylor, *Swords and Plowshares*

O NE OF THE most pivotal factors in America's failure in Vietnam was that it misjudged both the effectiveness of its own military strategy and the resolve of its enemy. The U.S. military's conventional methods of warfare had worked well in World War II, when the nation proved it was capable of successfully carrying out massive campaigns in Europe and Asia simultaneously. Its postwar military buildup resulting from the threat posed by the Soviets had created what was considered to be the largest and most powerful military force in the world. With this in mind, many considered early on that a conflict in Vietnam would bring certain victory. As former president Richard Nixon outlines in his book *No More Vietnams:*

> Seldom has one country enjoyed a superiority in arms greater than the United States held over North Vietnam in 1959. The war pitted a nuclear superpower with a gross national product [GNP] of $500 billion, armed forces numbering over 1 million, and a population of 180 million against a minor military power with a GNP of less than $2 billion, an army of 250,000, and a population of less than 16 million.[20]

U.S. soldiers in a South Vietnamese jungle consult their map. Unaccustomed to guerrilla warfare, American troops were at a distinct disadvantage in the jungles of Vietnam.

The American style of combat, however, had little effect against the tactics of the North Vietnamese Army and the Vietcong insurgents in South Vietnam, who often engaged in guerrilla warfare, literally translated as "little war," which had been successful against the French. They organized into small combat groups that moved rapidly and easily through the jungle terrain, evaded the heavy artillery and large battalions of the American military, and were capable of relying on far fewer supplies and logistical support than U.S. combat units. Thus, America's military found itself fighting in unfamiliar territory, surrounded by a population that could not be readily determined as friend or foe, and facing a battle-tested enemy.

A Hardened Enemy

In planning and prosecuting the Vietnam War, many U.S. political and military policy makers consistently underestimated the resolve of the North Vietnamese to continue the conflict. They failed to appreciate the history of the Vietnamese people, which was a tale of protracted warfare going back centuries. William J. Duiker in his biography *Ho Chi Minh* notes, "One of the lasting consequences of the Vietnamese struggle for national survival was undoubtedly the emergence of a strong military tradition and a willingness to use force to secure and protect national interests."[21] The Vietnamese had evolved into a nation of proud warriors, unintimidated by larger enemies like the Chinese and the French. To them, America was just one more invader to be repelled.

U.S. policy makers also did not learn the lessons of the French defeat in Vietnam in 1954. As George Ball reminded President Johnson in 1965, "The French fought a war in Vietnam, and were finally defeated—after seven years of bloody struggle and when they still had 250,000 combat-hardened veterans in the field, supported by an army of 205,000 South Vietnamese."[22]

In fighting the Americans, the NVA and the VC relied on their battle-tested guerilla tactics. They were experts in the art of camouflage, using tunnels and the dense jungle itself to disappear from advancing American forces. Sometimes the VC would infiltrate South Vietnamese villages where they blended in with the resident population, effectively hiding in plain sight. They were also skilled in tactical demolition and the application of booby traps that were responsible for killing and injuring thousands of unwary U.S. soldiers.

Another weapon the North Vietnamese skillfully applied in the war was patience. After combating the French colonial presence for generations, they learned to view final victory as a long-range, but inevitable, goal. They adapted their battlefield strategy accordingly, as Michael Lee Lanning and Dan Cragg note in *Inside the VC and the NVA: The Real Story of North Vietnam's Armed Forces:* "Tactical doctrine was explicit and can be summarized in four words: Four fast, one slow. This means fast advance, fast assault, fast clearance of the battlefield, and fast withdrawal—all based on slow preparation."[23]

The application of a patient guerrilla strategy was a marked contrast to the American fighting strategy, which emphasized action that resulted in enemy casualties and territory gained. From the start, the North did not intend to defeat the Americans on the battlefield, but only to maintain a viable combat force of their own until the United States tired of fighting. Ho displayed supreme confidence

The Tunnels of Cu Chi

The North Vietnamese Army (NVA) troops and the Vietcong dug thousands of miles of tunnels in the South during the war. This elaborate network stretched along the Ho Chi Minh Trail in Cambodia and throughout South Vietnam to the outskirts of Saigon itself. The tunnels hid supplies and troops from U.S. ground and aerial attack and also provided makeshift communication centers, bunkers, and hospitals.

In 1966 the U.S. 25th Infantry Division selected the area of Cu Chi as its headquarters because its topography was favorable during the monsoon season. Unbeknownst to the Americans, they had built their base on top of a Vietcong tunnel network. NVA captain Nguyen Thanh Linh explains the subsequent attack on the U.S. base in James William Gibson's *The Perfect War: Technowar in Vietnam:*

> "They [the Americans] were so bewildered, they did not hide or take defensive positions. They did not know where the bullets had come from. We kept on shooting. . . . Although their fellows kept falling down, they kept on advancing. They should have retreated. They called for artillery. When the first shells landed we simply went into the communications tunnels and went on to another place. The Americans continued advancing, but we'd gone."

A Vietcong soldier emerges from one of the thousands of underground tunnels at Cu Chi.

in this strategy when he remarked, "I think the Americans greatly underestimate the determination of the Vietnamese people."[24]

In Need of a New Strategy

In order to successfully combat the North Vietnamese, America had to change its whole strategic outlook. In the 1950s the United States based its defense policy on a reliance of massive military firepower to counteract Communist aggression. In response to Eisenhower's desire to cut defense spending while maintaining a strong military posture, the United States developed what became known as the "new look." This plan put much of the nation's strategic resources into the buildup of a devastating nuclear arsenal combined with an overwhelming air force bomber wing. Secretary of Defense John Foster Dulles, the architect of this strategy, believed that America could deter any Communist move with "massive retaliatory power . . . by means and places of our choosing."[25]

This doctrine of massive retaliation proved unworkable because, as Taylor, then army chief of staff, noted, "blasting [our enemies] from the face of the earth with atomic bombing . . . offers no alternative other than reciprocal suicide or retreat."[26] Upon entering office in January 1961, Kennedy was sympathetic to Taylor's assessment and found dire need for a strategy that offered more options than mutually assured destruction or surrender to counteract the Soviet threat. That same month Soviet premier Nikita Khrushchev had given a speech in Moscow in which he stated that the Soviet Union would support Communist insurgencies and revolutions anywhere in the world, including Vietnam.

Khrushchev's announcement prompted the United States to develop a doctrine of flexible response, in which military action could be geared to a level relative to the threat the country faced. In the case of Vietnam, flexible response meant providing logistical support to the ARVN and employing counterinsurgency tactics—small-scale warfare with conventional arms using traditional American fighting techniques.

When Westmoreland was appointed commander of U.S. forces in Vietnam in July 1964, he brought with him a three-phase plan that was consistent with the strategy of flexible response. First, American troops would develop and secure logistical bases throughout South Vietnam, particularly near the borders where NVA troops slipped

into the country. Second, U.S. and ARVN forces would attack and elim-
inate NVA and VC base camps and sanctuaries. The third and final
phase would consist of a major ground attack that would destroy the
enemy's main force or at least drive them out of the country.

There were several problems with this plan, not the least of which
was the utter lack of fighting ability of the ARVN. Beyond that, Westmoreland misread the country's topography and environment. American troops became mired down in the jungle, where the oppressive
heat, dampness, vegetation, snakes, and insects proved to be as formidable an enemy as the North Vietnamese.

The U.S. reliance on technology also worked against them. The
enemy learned to listen for and track helicopters, armored personnel
carriers, and the wake of patrol boats, and the VC were able to either
attack without warning or avoid detection altogether. Furthermore,
long-range artillery and air support proved largely ineffective in the
close-quarters combat in which Americans were often engaged.

Westmoreland's plan also ran into problems because it relied on
using more American troops than Washington was willing to provide.
This represented a larger disconnect that existed between military planners in the Joint Chiefs of Staff at the Pentagon and Johnson and his
civilian advisers in the White House. While the Joint Chiefs believed
that the war in Vietnam could only be won by full military commitment, Johnson was hesitant to send large numbers of troops to Southeast Asia. He feared widening the war by provoking the Soviets and
the Chinese, and he was also concerned about how such a commitment
would affect his domestic political agenda.

What was needed was a strategy that would address Johnson's concerns about widening the war but still provide an effective means of
stopping the Communists from taking over South Vietnam. It was
believed that graduated pressure was the answer.

The Argument over Graduated Pressure

The strategy of graduated pressure, as described by McMaster in *Dereliction of Duty,* "was not to impose one's will on the enemy but to communicate with him. Gradually intensifying military action would con-
vey American resolve and thereby convince an adversary to alter his
behavior."[27] The chief architect of this strategy was Secretary of Defense Robert S. McNamara.

General Westmoreland addresses soldiers in Saigon. Westmoreland's military strategy in Vietnam was largely a failure.

Kennedy appointed McNamara secretary of defense in 1961 because he thought McNamara was the perfect man to reorganize and modernize the sprawling American defense apparatus and its strategic thinking. McNamara possessed a brilliant analytical mind and had a solid reputation for applying new methods of statistical analysis in the private sector and as a strategic bombing analyst for the Army air force during World War II. McNamara's working style, however, did not endear him to the military establishment, and the strained relationship that developed had adverse consequences on the strategic planning for the war.

McNamara was given wide latitude by Kennedy to do what he needed to overhaul the Pentagon, and the new defense secretary exercised unprecedented civilian control over the department. He often discouraged dissent among his team of civilian analysts, known as the Whiz Kids, by ignoring any opinions or ideas that conflicted with his own. He also maintained strict privacy by rarely reporting to key subordinates what he was telling the president, or what the president was telling him. This exacerbated the mistrust the Joint Chiefs of Staff held for McNamara and his Whiz Kids, whom they viewed as civilian upstarts with no appreciation or knowledge of the military situation in Southeast Asia.

Defense Secretary Robert McNamara speaks with a U.S. soldier in Bien Hoa. McNamara proposed a plan that called for graduated military pressure in North Vietnam.

McNamara's plan called for measured strikes against military targets in North Vietnam and VC support bases in nearby Laos. Such strikes, as well as retaliatory actions by the U.S. and ARVN forces in the South, were meant to prevent the Communist government in Hanoi from continuing their support of the VC. It was made clear that these actions would have to be carefully calculated to prevent an escalation of hostilities or erosion of international and domestic support for the war. The plan did not clearly define at what level such reactions would take place, but McNamara believed that, if properly executed, it would offer the United States an "acceptable outcome within a reasonable time."[28]

Taylor, then chairman of the Joint Chiefs of Staff, agreed with McNamara's assessment, and together the two men kept the Joint Chiefs out of the decision-making process to prevent their opposing views from reaching Johnson. Air force general Curtis LeMay, Admiral David Lamar McDonald, and Marine Corps commandant General Wallace Greene all expressed doubts over graduated pressure, referring to it as a half-measure that would not achieve victory in Vietnam. "We are swatting flies when we ought to be going after the manure pile,"[29] LeMay said. He and his colleagues believed that only a hard, concentrated attack on North Vietnam would bring an end to their support of the Communist insurgency in the South.

The civilian leaders in Washington felt that graduated pressure was the answer. Rusk felt the plan would never give China or Russia "enough of a change in the situation to require them to make a major decision . . . in terms of intervening."[30] Johnson supported the plan because it answered his questions about how to demonstrate America's commitment to stop the spread of communism in Southeast Asia without escalating the fight into a world war. It also called for less than a full-scale military commitment, allowing Johnson to focus government resources on his coveted domestic legislative agenda.

Thus graduated pressure became more of a political solution than a military one. It solved short-term problems for the administration,

---

 ## The Phoenix Program

The secret program known as Phoenix was a joint U.S.–South Vietnamese plan to strike a severe blow against the Vietcong infiltrators in the South. The definition, scope, and drawbacks of this action are described in Douglas Valentine's *The Phoenix Program:*

> Developed in 1967 by the Central Intelligence Agency (CIA), Phoenix combined existing counterinsurgency programs in a concerted effort to "neutralize" the Vietcong infrastructure (VCI). The euphemism "neutralize" means to kill, capture, or make to defect. The word "infrastructure" refers to those civilians suspected of supporting the North Vietnamese and Vietcong. . . . Central to Phoenix is the fact that it targeted civilians, not soldiers.

> South Vietnamese civilians whose names appeared on blacklists could be kidnapped, tortured, detained for two years without trial, or even murdered. . . . At its height Phoenix managers imposed quotas of eighteen hundred neutralizations per month . . . opening up the program to abuses by corrupt security officials, policemen, politicians, and racketeers. . . .

> Phoenix proponents describe the program as a "scalpel" designed to replace the "bludgeon" of search and destroy operations, air strikes, and artillery barrages that indiscriminately wiped out entire villages and did little to "win the hearts and minds" of the Vietnamese population.

but it did not address long-term concerns about how the United States intended to ultimately defeat the North Vietnamese and keep the South safe from a Communist takeover.

Rolling Thunder Falls Short

A principal element of the graduated pressure strategy was the sustained bombing of VC bases in the South and installations in North Vietnam, a campaign known as Operation Rolling Thunder. The Joint Chiefs wanted a stronger air presence to protect American soldiers in the field and cut the supply lines to the NVA and VC forces in the South. Johnson and his civilian war planners felt a demonstration of force was needed to shore up the confidence of the South Vietnamese and break the will of the North Vietnamese. After a VC raid killed eight American servicemen at the U.S. military installation at Pleiku on February 6, 1965, in the central highlands, Johnson gave the order to commence Operation Rolling Thunder.

The Rolling Thunder campaign was designed to strike NVA and VC targets on a regular schedule that was meant to escalate until the North withdrew its forces from South Vietnam. The campaign, originally conceived to be an eight-week program, lasted from March 1965 until 1968 and met with only limited success for a variety of reasons. Johnson, ever wary of provoking a retaliatory response from China and Russia in defense of North Vietnam, insisted on running the bombing campaign from the White House. He placed strict rules of engagement on American aircraft, effectively barring them from operating near the Chinese border, in and around Hanoi, or the port at Haiphong—all key areas of logistical and strategic support for the North Vietnamese. A list of other potential targets drawn up by the Pentagon was submitted to the White House each week for Johnson, McNamara, Rusk, and national security adviser McGeorge Bundy to review and approve. This led to long delays in choosing targets, the choice of strategically unimportant targets, and many missed opportunities.

Allowing such direct control over the battlefield from such a remote and isolated location created a host of problems. At the start of the campaign Westmoreland wrote General Earl Wheeler, then chairman of the Joint Chiefs, "The more remote the authority which directs how a mission is to be accomplished, the more we are vulnerable to

F-105 fighters escort a B-66 in a bombing raid over North Vietnam in 1966. Operation Rolling Thunder, the bombing campaign that lasted from 1965 to 1968, had limited success.

mishaps resulting from such things as incomplete briefings and preparation, loss of tactical flexibility and lack of tactical coordination."[31]

Infrequent pauses in the bombing also stalled the momentum that could have been gained by continued U.S. military pressure. Johnson declared a bombing halt during Christmas 1965 in hope of bringing North Vietnam to the negotiating table. Hanoi refused to negotiate, instead taking advantage of the pause to rebuild destroyed roads, bridges, and facilities, and to move troops and supplies into the South. Johnson called for seven more bombing pauses during the Rolling Thunder campaign, and each pause met with the same results. Rather than give in to Johnson's offer to exchange a negotiated settlement for a full bombing halt, Ho declared that the United States "must stop its air attacks on the North, put an end to its aggression in the South; withdraw its troops from South Vietnam; and let the Vietnamese people settle themselves their own affairs."[32]

There was no desire for the North Vietnamese to negotiate because, despite the heavy bombing, they did not feel they were in such a position of weakness to attempt settlement. This was due partly to the signals sent by the American air effort. While the White House believed the bombing was communicating American resolve to defend South Vietnam, Hanoi interpreted the bombing pauses as a sign of indecision and confusion on the part of the Americans.

Nor did the bombing inflict significant enough damage to hamper the North's war effort. The country had a primarily agrarian economy, so there was little industry to destroy. Much of their war matériel came from China and the Soviet Union.

The adaptability of the North Vietnamese also lessened the effects of the bombing campaign. Hoopes describes an example of this in *The Limits of Intervention:* "U.S. aircraft had knocked out a small railroad bridge outside of Hanoi. The whole population of the nearby village was herded together and each person was told to fill his rice bag with dirt. One by one, the 1,000-odd bags were piled up to fill the bomb crater. New railroad tracks were laid on top and trains were moving again within twenty-four hours."[33]

Such ingenuity and obstinacy on the part of the North Vietnamese led Wheeler to remark, "Outwardly, the North Vietnamese government appears to be uninfluenced by our air strikes."[34] Even McNamara had come to believe that Hanoi could not be bombed into negotiations.

In the summer of 1966 McNamara commissioned a study by the Institute for Defense Analysis on the effectiveness of Rolling Thunder. In their final analysis it was determined that "the Rolling Thunder program clearly tended to overestimate the persuasive and disruptive effects of the U.S. air strikes, and, correspondingly, to underestimate the tenacity and recuperative abilities of the North Vietnamese."[35]

During the three years of Rolling Thunder, U.S. Air Force and Navy bombers dropped over South and North Vietnam nine times the tonnage expended throughout the Pacific during World War II. This staggering toll amounted to seventy tons for every square mile, or five hundred pounds for every man, woman, and child in Vietnam; yet it had little effect on the North Vietnamese war effort.

 **The Ho Chi Minh Trail**

The principal route for North Vietnamese troops and supplies, known to both North and South as the Ho Chi Minh Trail, ran through Laos and Cambodia along the South Vietnamese border, crossing into that nation at several points. Growing out of a loose connection of trails and roads, the Trail became a complex supply system of primary and secondary roads that remained operational throughout the war, even under ever-increasing American air strikes.

Michael Lee Lanning and Dan Cragg explain the extent of the Trail's importance to the North Vietnamese war effort in *Inside the VC and the NVA: The Real Story of North Vietnam's Armed Forces:*

> [After 1964] the subsequent high rate of traffic on the Ho Chi Minh Trail is reflected by the growing numbers of NVA soldiers in the South. In 1964 the number was only 6,000. By 1967 this number had grown to 69,000 and to over 100,000 by 1969. Considering replacements for casualties, as well as new units committed to the war, at the height of the conflict, the Trail was the route for as many as 60,000 infiltrators per year.

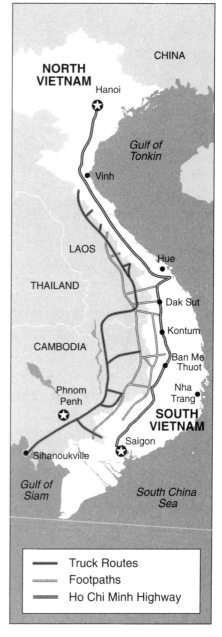

— Truck Routes
= Footpaths
= Ho Chi Minh Highway

A U.S. soldier places a wounded Vietcong prisoner on a stretcher. The large number of North Vietnamese POWs and casualties led the U.S. government to believe victory was inevitable.

The Numbers Game

The careful management of bombing targets and the statistical measurement of the multitude of bombing sorties flown is an example of how America attempted to quantify success in Vietnam. Engaging in a war unlike any it had ever fought, the United States found itself unsure of how to achieve victory. Johnson demanded to know on a regular basis whether the war effort was making any progress. McNamara in turn demanded weekly reports from the American military command in Vietnam.

The commanders had no way to determine progress in terms of the week-to-week success or failure of the U.S. mission in Vietnam, so both civilian and military leaders devised methods of calculating military progress in Vietnam. Military analysts counted the number of weapons captured from or abandoned by NVA and VC soldiers, which they determined as a measure of success in that seized guns, ammunition, and artillery steadily increased throughout the war. They also counted the number of enemy deserters, as well as the number of civilians and total territory under South Vietnamese control. By far the most outlandish quantifier of all was the body count.

The military commanders in the field, like their superiors in Washington, believed the total number of enemy dead in comparison to American dead was the surest measure of success or failure in Vietnam. After battles, U.S. troops would go out on body-counting missions to determine how many VC had been killed. This was many times a dangerous affair because enemy snipers would sometimes linger behind after their main force had retreated. A U.S. Army training manual explains the dangers of one such body counting mission: "The skipper sends out a four-man patrol to police weapons and count bodies. Three men return bearing the fourth, who was wounded before the job was well started. Another patrol was sent. The same thing happened."[36]

The North Vietnamese did suffer comparatively higher casualties than the American military, but this information, like many other numbers that were gathered, was misleading. The techniques used to measure these statistics were crude, untested, and there was no reliable way to verify their validity. Also, the military tended to skew numbers in a favorable direction, erring on the side of optimism when they could not accurately determine a particular count. Some officers looking to project an image of success and advance their careers even manipulated the figures.

The number of enemy casualties encouraged Johnson and the Pentagon to believe that the United States was in fact winning the war. Tactical battlefield successes against the NVA in the Ia Drang Valley and at Chu Lai in 1965 and Dak To in 1967 gave Westmoreland reason to be optimistic about America's ability to prevail. Yet the North Vietnamese could not be forced to either quit or negotiate.

The escalating number of U.S. casualties also forced the American public and some policy makers in Washington to reevaluate their support for the struggle. From 1960 to 1966 there were a total of 7,500 American servicemen killed in action; that number jumped to over 9,000 in 1967 alone, with another 60,000 wounded. Neither Johnson nor his closest advisers could find a way to scale back America's involvement without completely abandoning South Vietnam, which in itself was a move no one was willing to make.

A Disillusioned Leadership

Chapter 3

The war was a vampire sucking dry the administration's vitality.

—Undersecretary of State George Ball, quoted in *Guns or Butter: The Presidency of Lyndon Johnson* by Irving Bernstein

THE BELIEF THAT the United States could prevail in Vietnam despite mounting evidence to the contrary was one that was tightly held by Johnson and his core group of advisers. This was a flaw mainly of Johnson's own making, in that he had an inherent inability to accept advice that ran counter to his own views. He placed such a high value on loyalty that he often interpreted disagreement as betrayal. He was at odds with the Joint Chiefs of Staff for this reason, and even came to mistrust his civilian advisers, many of whom lost confidence in the effort as the war dragged on.

Johnson was also monumentally indecisive about the level of commitment he wanted to project in Southeast Asia. He had pledged to prevent South Vietnam from falling to the Communists from the time he took office. Just days after Kennedy's death on November 22, 1963, Johnson told Lodge, the ambassador to South Vietnam, "I'm not going to lose Vietnam. I am not going to be the president who saw Southeast Asia go the way China went."[37] Johnson, however, was constantly worried about escalating the conflict, and he insisted on running the war from the White House despite his own lack of military experience. Johnson's indecision and mistrust resulted in America postponing defeat rather than pursuing victory. Johnson's presidency and the men who served it would pay a high price for this shortcoming, as would the rest of the nation.

Fighting the War on a Campaign Schedule

Johnson endeavored for as seamless a transition to the presidency as possible following Kennedy's assassination. His first actions in this regard included signing a National Security Council memorandum stating that the United States would help South Vietnam "win their contest against the externally directed and supported Communist conspiracy."[38] This assured the continuation of U.S. military assistance, which included $500 million in aid and over sixteen thousand military advisers in 1963 alone.

President Johnson expresses frustration as McNamara briefs him on news from Vietnam in 1964. Johnson remained convinced that, despite setbacks, the United States would prevail in Vietnam.

Johnson also kept many of Kennedy's advisers, including McNamara, Bundy, Rusk, and many others. "You're men I trust the most. You must stay with me. I'll need you,"[39] Johnson told them. And indeed, he would. For all his years in politics, Johnson had never developed a strong sense of the intricacies of foreign policy, and many intellectuals of the time thought he had a limited worldview that would hamper international relations.

Despite being unskilled in foreign affairs, Johnson was politically shrewd and very much possessed with earning the presidency in his own right rather than by the death of his predecessor. With the 1964 presidential election approaching, Johnson was willing to portray himself in whatever fashion that would get him reelected. His opponent, Republican senator Barry Goldwater, favored a tough stance with the Soviets. Goldwater was very much a hawk, stating during his acceptance speech at the Republican National Convention in July, "Extremism in the defense of liberty is no vice."[40]

Many Americans feared that Goldwater would lead the United States into a catastrophic war and possibly even a nuclear exchange with the Soviet Union and the Chinese over Vietnam. In response, Johnson actively sought the image of a moderate candidate. "We are not going to send American boys nine or ten thousand miles around the

---

The Gulf of Tonkin Resolution

Despite doubts surrounding a second attack on U.S. ships by North Vietnamese patrol boats in the Gulf of Tonkin in August 1964, Johnson received overwhelming congressional approval for a resolution giving him virtually unlimited authority to wage war against North Vietnam. The heart of the resolution, as quoted in Irving Bernstein's *Guns or Butter: The Presidency of Lyndon Johnson*, stated:

> The United States regards as vital to its national interest and to world peace the maintenance of international peace and security in Southeast Asia. Consonant with the Constitution of the United States . . . and in accordance with its obligations under the Southeast Asia Collective Defense Treaty, the United States is, therefore, prepared, as the President determines, to take all necessary steps, including the use of armed force, to assist any member or protocol state of the Southeast Asia Collective Defense Treaty requiring assistance in defense of its freedom.

world to be doing a job that Asian boys ought to be doing for themselves,"[41] Johnson told audiences on the campaign trail. Even though this statement was counter to the U.S. policy of the time, it demonstrates the extent to which Johnson's decisions were affected by his bellicose opponent.

During this time the White House had authorized Operation Plan 34A, a series of covert actions against North Vietnam. These actions included reconnaissance flights over the North, kidnappings of army officers, sabotage, and the insertion of psychological warfare teams into the country. McNamara presented the plan to Johnson, noting that it offered a "wide variety of sabotage and psychological operations against North Vietnam from which I believe we should aim to select those that provide maximum pressure with minimum risk."[42] Johnson readily approved it. A draft resolution was also being prepared for submission to Congress that would grant Johnson the authority to engage in open-ended military action in Vietnam. It was determined that there was not enough congressional approval for such a measure, so the resolution was put aside, but the covert operations went ahead.

On July 31, 1964, as part of Operation Plan 34A, South Vietnamese speedboats attacked two North Vietnamese radar installations in the Gulf of Tonkin. Two days later three North Vietnamese patrol boats attacked the USS *Maddox,* a destroyer in the vicinity at the time of the raids. No Americans were injured, and one of the patrol boats was sunk by American planes from the nearby aircraft carrier *Ticonderoga.*

Johnson opted against retaliation, fearing that instigating a wider conflict would run counter to his stance as a moderate in the presidential race. The raids in the Gulf of Tonkin continued, however, and the American naval presence in the region increased substantially with the addition of the USS *Turner Joy* and another aircraft carrier. On August 3 there were reports of another attack by the North Vietnamese, but poor weather obscured American surveillance equipment, and the validity of the attack could not be determined. Skipper of the *Maddox* John J. Herrick summed up the confusion of the situation: "The [USS *Turner*] *Joy* was firing at 'targets' the *Maddox* couldn't track on radar, and the *Maddox* was dodging 'torpedoes' the *Joy* couldn't hear on sonar."[43]

There were no credible witnesses to this second attack, but word of it spread rapidly. The American public demanded a response, and

Johnson had to appear decisive, particularly in comparison with Goldwater's hawkish supporters. A retaliatory bombing strike against several targets in North Vietnam was agreed upon. Johnson wanted to time his televised announcement of the air strikes with the execution of the bombing runs. Due to the twelve-hour time difference between Washington and Hanoi, Johnson ended up going on the air at midnight, announcing to the American people that the U.S. response to the attack would be measured, and that he did not want to widen the conflict.

After the raids Johnson turned to Congress, requesting approval for further American military action in Vietnam. The resolution that was submitted received overwhelming support, passing the House unanimously and clearing the Senate by all but two votes.

Johnson's public commitment to a measured involvement in Vietnam won wide support with the public. He defeated Goldwater in the 1964 presidential race by 16 million votes, the largest electoral landslide in American history up to that time. Democrats also gained a two-to-one majority over Republicans in Congress. With the election victory and the Gulf of Tonkin Resolution, which granted the president authority to wage war against North Vietnam Johnson possessed a solid mandate to prosecute the war. However, as the war dragged on, and Johnson's public and political supporters grew weary of it, that mandate began to fall apart.

Dissension in the Ranks

Most of Johnson's civilian advisory team held strong convictions about the political implications of America's involvement in Southeast Asia. They subscribed to the "domino theory" and believed that the fall of South Vietnam would endanger all of Southeast Asia. Rusk framed their concerns: "The integrity of the U.S. commitment is the principal pillar of peace throughout the world. If that commitment becomes unreliable, the communist world would draw conclusions that would lead to our ruin and almost certainly to a catastrophic war."[44]

The one notable opponent to escalation in Vietnam was Ball. He was wary of U.S. troops getting sucked into a protracted conflict in the jungle, noting to his White House colleagues, "What we might gain by establishing the steadfastness of our commitments, we could lose by an erosion of confidence in our judgements."[45]

Ball's advice was often ignored by the other men on Johnson's team, but the president wanted him to remain on board. Johnson sought to maintain the image that he was listening to all sides of the war debate when he was not. In fact, there was really not much of a debate at all, and consultation over strategy was confined to this small group of insiders who insulated the president from adverse opinions.

Walt Rostow, one of Johnson's more militant advisers, noted that in the weekly meetings held to discuss Vietnam, "the only men present were those whose advice the president most wanted to hear."[46] And for all the military strategy that was discussed at these sessions, there was rarely a military officer in the room.

President Johnson (far right) meets with George Ball (second from left) and other advisers. Although most of Johnson's advisers agreed with his strategy, Ball was wary of a protracted war in Vietnam.

The Joint Chiefs of Staff, which had split from the administration over the application of McNamara's graduated pressure strategy, was often removed from the decision-making process. Within the Pentagon, the Joint Chiefs fought among themselves, each believing that his own respective military branch was best suited to handle the mission in Vietnam. When they could reach consensus, McNamara routinely suppressed their advice to the president and buried their recommendations. This was detrimental to the war effort in that the administration was cut off from viable alternatives that the Joint Chiefs could have provided in strategic planning.

An example of how the suppression of information harmed the American mission in Vietnam was the Sigma I 64 war game. Conducted by the Joint Chiefs, this exercise assigned roles to Bundy, Wheeler, LeMay, and others. They applied different levels of military pressure on a fictional North Vietnam in a variety of scenarios. In the end, they determined that several hundred thousand U.S. troops would be required over the course of several years to achieve even moderate success in the South. The war game results also predicted that domestic support would disintegrate over time, making the military commitment more difficult to maintain. This information would have proved invaluable to Johnson's strategic planning, but due to its negative nature it was restricted and never reached his desk.

As the results of the Sigma war game slowly became reality, the president's once solid base of support among his advisers began to fall apart. When Taylor was chairman of the Joint Chiefs, he had been a strong supporter of the military commitment in South Vietnam. After spending a year in South Vietnam as the American ambassador, his views changed. "I had become convinced that we were going too slow in the application of military power, air and ground, to accomplish our intended purposes."[47] Johnson came to value Taylor's input less after this realization.

Despite sending more troops and dropping more bombs, America made little progress in Vietnam. Upon returning from a trip to South Vietnam McNamara submitted a report to Johnson on October 14, 1966, reflecting serious concerns about the situation. "Enemy morale has not broken—he apparently has adjusted to our stopping his drive for military victory and has adopted a strategy of keeping us busy and waiting us out. . . . Nor has the Rolling Thunder program of bombing the North either significantly affected infiltration or cracked the morale of Hanoi."[48]

 **The San Antonio Formula**

Almost from the start of the extended American bombing campaign against North Vietnam, Johnson hoped to draw the Communists to the negotiating table through brief bombing pauses but the North rejected each overture.

On September 29, 1967, Johnson introduced in a speech what came to be known as the San Antonio Formula, an administration plan to use a sustained halt in the bombing to establish a dialogue with Hanoi that would lead to constructive talks. Johnson, as quoted in Gardner's *Pay Any Price*, stated:

> As we have told Hanoi time and time and time again, the heart of the matter is really this: The United States is willing to stop all aerial and naval bombardment of North Vietnam when this will lead promptly to productive discussions. We, of course, assume that while discussions proceed, North Vietnam would not take advantage of the bombing cessation or limitation.

This statement was the most candid attempt by Johnson in the pursuit of peace to date, but it was resolutely rejected by the North Vietnamese, who considered the offer insulting.

This information, and the growing opposition of some of his most trusted aides, did not sway Johnson from his belief that the United States could hold the line against the Communists. The Tet Offensive of 1968, however, brought a sudden end to any illusions about impending American victory in Vietnam.

Tet: A Successful Failure for North Vietnam

Growing U.S. intelligence pointed to a major offensive during the 1968 Tet holiday, which was the Vietnamese New Year. Both South and North Vietnam had observed a cease-fire during the 1967 holiday, but troops, supplies, and ammunition had been massing along the Ho Chi Minh Trail, a vast network of roads leading from North Vietnam into the South, and Westmoreland believed an assault was soon coming.

The offensive had been envisioned years before in Hanoi. General Vo Nguyen Giap, a longtime colleague of Ho Chi Minh who became commander of the North Vietnamese armed forces, noted in 1965 that to ensure success, "it is necessary to promote an extensive guerilla war which will develop gradually into a regular war."[49] By laying siege to

A South Vietnamese family flees from the fighting during the Tet offensive in January 1968. The surprise attack caught the U.S. military almost completely off guard.

the American base at Khe Sahn and launching diversionary strikes in late 1967 to scatter American forces along the demilitarized zone and in the Mekong Delta, the North believed they had created the opportunity to launch Giap's "regular war."

This change in strategy was brought on by the massive American military buildup in South Vietnam, which Hanoi recognized could delay their plans for conquest of the South indefinitely. It was their intention to launch an offensive that would both demoralize the American war effort and inspire open revolt in the South by demonstrating to the South Vietnamese that their government was ineffective and could not protect them. The element of surprise was the North's most potent weapon.

On January 30, 1968, the eve of Tet, over eighty thousand Vietcong, supported by troops from the North Vietnamese Army, launched a massive assault across South Vietnam, catching American forces almost completely unawares. Thirty-five NVA and VC battalions swarmed into Saigon, attacking the presidential palace and the American embassy. In the ancient city of Hue twenty-eight hundred teachers, government officials, and intellectuals were murdered for their suspected collaboration with the South Vietnamese government. In total, thirty-nine provincial capitals and seventy-one district towns in the country were attacked, with the focus on government and military installations, political offices, and administrative centers.

Within eight weeks American and ARVN forces were able to beat back the offensive nationwide, losing 3,800 and 5,000 men, respectively. The siege at Khe Sahn was lifted on April 8 with the help of U.S. aircraft, which dropped over 100,000 tons of bombs and expended 700,000 rounds of ammunition on NVA positions. The North Vietnamese were reported to have suffered over 58,000 casualties during Tet, a figure that has never been verified but is considered plausible by historians.

South Vietnam maintained control over all the territory it possessed prior to the offensive, and the Vietcong were effectively decimated as a fighting force. No popular uprising among the peasants occurred as Hanoi had hoped yet the American public's resoundingly negative reaction to Tet gave them the psychological victory they were seeking.

Domestic support for involvement in Vietnam eroded after the Tet Offensive. Many who had been led to believe by the Johnson administration that America was winning the war came to see Vietnam as a hopeless endeavor because the deployment of hundreds of thousands of American soldiers and the tens of thousands of combat deaths had made no fundamental change in the situation. After this point, the president's popularity rapidly disintegrated. Walter Cronkite, considered to be the most respected newsman in America, encapsulated the general public view when he said, "It seems more certain than ever that the bloody experience in Vietnam is to end in a stalemate."[50] By this point Johnson had reached the limit of his abilities to steer America through Vietnam.

The Demise of Lyndon Johnson

After the Tet Offensive Johnson's approval rating in the polls plunged to 36 percent; support for his handling of the war was down to 26 percent. During his five years in office he had authorized the increase of American combat forces in Vietnam from 16,000 to 550,000, and yet the United States was no closer to victory. The cost of the war had risen from $103 million in 1965 to $25 billion in 1968, causing inflation and economic instability at home.

Johnson's congressional support likewise evaporated as more people turned against the war. With few friends in Congress and the cost of the war weighing heavily on the federal budget, his treasured domestic plan, known as the Great Society, lay unfinished.

Johnson had first outlined the Great Society in his 1964 State of the Union address, and hoped to use government resources to alleviate poverty, reduce crime, clean up the inner cities, and pass meaningful civil rights legislation. While he was able to achieve parts of this ambitious agenda, he could have accomplished much more were it not for the high cost of the war in Vietnam. "Losing the Great Society was a terrible thought," Johnson told biographer Doris Kearns, "but not so terrible as the thought of being responsible for America's losing a war to the Communists."[51]

With political and public support at an all-time low, Johnson's inner circle fell apart. Ball and Bundy had departed in 1966 to pursue other endeavors. Both men had recognized the inability to achieve victory in Vietnam and could no longer bear the burden of trying. Robert McNamara, the man most responsible for crafting the administration's Vietnam policy, had become likewise disillusioned. He told the pres-

 **The Wise Men**

In October 1967 a group of senior statesmen gathered to assess the situation in Vietnam and offer Johnson their advice on the matter. Among them were Dean Acheson, secretary of state and architect of early Cold War policy for Truman; five-star general Omar Bradley; under secretary of state George Ball; national security adviser McGeorge Bundy; former treasury secretary Douglas Dillon; diplomat Averell Harriman; and former ambassadors to South Vietnam Henry Cabot Lodge and General Maxwell Taylor.

This group of "wise men," as they were nicknamed, were among the top minds in the Washington political establishment. When they recommended that Johnson hold firm on his present course of action in Vietnam, he felt vindicated in his decision to continue the American military engagement.

When the group convened again the following March, however, opinions had changed. Bundy, Acheson, Ball, Dean, and others believed that America was paying too high a price for what had become a stalemate in Southeast Asia and recommended a steady disengagement from the region. Johnson was deeply upset by this change of course among his most respected advisers and felt the burden of having only a few supporters left.

ident "point-blank, that we could not achieve our objective in Vietnam through any reasonable military means. . . . President Johnson was not ready to accept that. It was becoming clear to both of us that I would not change my judgement, nor would he change his. Something had to give."[52] McNamara submitted his resignation and left the administration on February 29, 1968.

On March 12 the New Hampshire Democratic primary signaled the start of the 1968 presidential race. Minnesota senator Eugene McCarthy, running as an antiwar Democrat, lost to the incumbent Johnson by only three hundred votes, signifying the division that existed within the party over the war. Four days later the hugely popular New York senator Robert Kennedy joined the race, calling for an end to the war.

Johnson, haggard from his time in office, defeated by Vietnam, and worn out from the extreme stress of his job, confided to his wife, Lady Bird, "I do not believe I can unite this country."[53] On March 31, 1968, Johnson made a televised address to the nation, announcing a

During his last months in office in 1968, President Johnson concentrated on trying to negotiate a peace settlement with the North Vietnamese.

bombing halt to urge Hanoi to begin peace talks. The words he chose to close his address stunned the nation:

> With America's sons in the fields so far away, with America's future under challenge right here at home, with our hopes and the world's hopes for peace in the balance every day, I do not believe that I should devote an hour or a day of my time to any personal partisan causes or to any duties other than the awesome duties of this office—the Presidency of your country.

> Accordingly, I shall not seek, and I will not accept, the nomination of my party for another term as your President.[54]

Johnson spent his remaining months in office working to negotiate peace with the North Vietnamese, but they procrastinated on the details in the hope of gaining a better deal as the American position in the South continued to erode.

For his part, Johnson operated from a position of weakness for a number of reasons. His poor management of the war had left the American military in a stalemate against the North Vietnamese. His most capable and trusted advisers had departed the administration, leaving him less informed and politically isolated. And the American public's weariness with the war had led to massive demonstrations and widespread unrest throughout the country. As a consequence, Johnson bequeathed an unwinnable and unfinished war to his successor, as well as an America wracked by internal strife of a magnitude not experienced since the Civil War.

Chapter 4 The War at Home

The violence in Vietnam seemed to elicit a similar air of violence in the United States, an appetite for extremes: people felt that history was accelerating, time was running out.
—Thomas Powers, journalist

T HE AMERICAN PEOPLE shared the frustration and disillusionment that existed within the Johnson administration over the stalemate in Vietnam. While a majority of the public supported the war effort in 1964 and 1965, the mounting U.S. casualties and rising financial cost of the conflict forced many to reevaluate their position. Johnson recognized that he could not continue the war without the backing of the American people, but his inability to maintain congressional support or effectively communicate the country's mission in Southeast Asia to the public alienated the war-weary nation. As it became apparent that victory could not be achieved in Vietnam despite growing U.S. involvement, opposition to the war grew.

This discord over Vietnam came during a time of great political and social change in the United States. The 1960s saw the convergence of a number of movements that were working to advance the rights and living standards of blacks, Hispanics, women, the urban poor, and migrant workers. On college and university campuses, the nation's youth were becoming politically active like never before, seeking to bring change to a system they saw as corrupt and rigged by an establishment that controlled business and government institutions. It was this establishment, real or imagined, that was blamed by activists of all persuasions for the debacle in Vietnam.

The growing disconnect from mainstream society felt by students and minorities led them to rely on more combative and violent methods of showing opposition to the war. Writer and activist Norman Mailer reflected the resilience of the antiwar movement at a University of California at Berkeley demonstration in 1965: "[The protestors] will go on marches and they will make demonstrations, and they will begin a

A group of female activists in Washington, D.C., demonstrates against the war in Vietnam. As casualties in Vietnam mounted, the antiwar movement in the United States gained momentum.

war of public protest against you which will never cease. It will go on and on and it will get stronger and stronger."[55]

Radical Opposition

The antiwar groups grew from the actions of a few dedicated protesters into a nationwide movement that slowly turned the tide of public opinion against involvement in Vietnam. Johnson believed that the antiwar protestors were boosting morale in North Vietnam and were being guided by the Communists. While the former may have been true, no proof was ever provided of the latter. Both the Central Intelligence Agency and the State Department undertook studies into the matter and concluded that there was no tangible connection between the Communist conspiracy and the antiwar movement. The State Department study noted, "The Communist role in student unrest is considerably more often alleged than confirmed."[56] By rejecting the fact that the antiwar movement was a homegrown phenomenon, Johnson passed up the opportunity early on to gain an understanding of public sentiment.

 **Dodging the Draft**

From 1964 to 1973 over 1.5 million men were drafted into the U.S. military to serve in Vietnam. These draftees were statistically more likely than volunteers to die in combat due to their placement in high-risk areas and their comparative lack of fighting skill.

Many young men publicly burned their draft cards or fled the nation in protest. One group that resisted the draft was the May 2nd Movement, which posted the following ad in the *New York Herald Tribune*, quoted in *Vietnam and America* by Marvin E. Gettleman, et al.:

> We the undersigned, are young Americans of draft age. We understand our obligations to defend our country and to serve in the armed forces but we object to being asked to support the war in South Vietnam.
>
> Believing that United States' participation in the war is for the suppression of the Vietnamese struggle for national independence, we see no justification for our involvement. . . .
>
> Believing that we should not be asked to fight against the people of Vietnam, we herewith state our refusal to do so.

Groups like Students for a Democratic Society (SDS), the Student Nonviolent Coordinating Committee, and the Free Speech Movement at UC–Berkeley focused their energies toward bringing an end to the war and ending what they believed was government influence in America's university system.

These groups grew more radical as they grew in size. SDS, being a student organization, was subject to an annual turnover, with each new leadership group replacing recent graduates and coming in at a later stage in the movement. They were influenced by increasingly chaotic events and further unraveling of the social fabric in the country, which, in turn, made them more radical.

As the war escalated despite widespread marches, sit-ins, and student strikes, many of these youth leaders believed they had to resort to bolder actions in order to be heard. By 1967 one SDS leader, Carl Davidson, believed that the time had come to abandon earlier tactics for a new strategy to carry out the "disruption, dislocation, and destruction of the military's access to the manpower, intelligence, or resources of our universities."[57]

From this point forward demonstrations grew more chaotic, with students burning draft cards, getting into fights with police, and seizing administrative buildings at Columbia University, UC–Berkeley, Harvard, and other schools. Reserve Officer Training Corps (ROTC) offices on college campuses, which had been the target of criticism and protest, came under outright attack and were subject to vandalism and arson. The conduct of the demonstrators caused alarm in mainstream America, where many believed that it was the antiwar movement that was tearing the country apart, not the war in Southeast Asia. Senator Gordon Allott of Colorado warned of "an active, aggressive national conspiracy to destroy by force and violence, including the use of dangerous weapons, the peace and dignity of the academic communities."[58]

Antiwar rallies numbering in the tens of thousands continued to sprout up in major cities across the country. Among the most notable of these events were the November 1965 gathering in which thirty-five thousand demonstrators circled the White House; the New York City march on May 13, 1967, which drew seventy thousand; and the October 31, 1967, march on the Pentagon, in which over fifty thousand antiwar demonstrators attempted to shut down the massive military complex.

The movement was no longer confined to just the college-aged population, either. Martin Luther King Jr., whose work in obtaining civil rights for African Americans had earned him the Nobel Peace Prize, became involved in the antiwar movement. He made notice of the many young black men who were being drafted to fight and die in Vietnam for a country whose government would not even grant them the basic rights whites had enjoyed for so long. "I knew I could never again raise my voice against the violence of the repressed in the ghettos without having first spoken clearly to the greatest purveyor of violence in the world today—my own government."[59]

King's demands were the same as the students': Stop the bombing in Vietnam, enact a unilateral cease-fire, and bring the troops home without delay. However, his strategy of civil disobedience was no longer suited to the more militant members of the civil rights movement, who had now taken to confrontation rather than cooperation to achieve their goals.

Civil rights legislation had not conquered the problems of racial inequality and poverty in black America, and the promise of the Great Society had been cut short to help defray the cost of the war. Men like Stokley Carmichael and Huey P. Newton of the Black Panthers sought broader change in a shorter period of time. Their rallying cry— Black Power—energized blacks with a fierce sense of pride in the African culture and history of their ancestors and unnerved whites around the country. Riots in Harlem, Philadelphia, Los Angeles, Chicago, Cleveland, and dozens of other cities exacerbated racial tensions. King's assassination on April 4, 1968, pushed these tensions past the breaking point as violence erupted simultaneously in over a hundred cities.

The violence that was associated with the black power movement and the antiwar movement in the late 1960s prevented them from achieving their respective goals in any fundamental way, but it did have an effect on the wider public's view of the war. Jeffrey Kimball reflects on the impact of the antiwar movement in *Nixon's Vietnam War*:

What few restraints the Johnson administration had imposed on their military effort had been as much, if not more than antiwar protest, the product of other concerns: the economic price . . . of greater and more rapid escalation; the impact of a

Anti-war student protesters in Virginia clash with police in 1967. As they grew in size, some student organizations adopted radical tactics in their efforts to halt the war in Vietnam.

larger commitment in Vietnam upon America's global posture; and . . . Soviet and Chinese responses. . . . The majority of the public came to dislike street-demonstration tactics more than they disliked the war itself. . . . On the other hand . . . the words and actions of the protestors contributed to their general war weariness. "The dissidents did not stop the war," one historian of the movement argued, "but they did make it stoppable."[60]

Congressional Criticism

While Congress had demonstrated almost unanimous support for the Gulf of Tonkin Resolution in 1964, they could not ignore the growing unrest in the streets of America's cities. Even as the war dragged on with no evident resolution in sight, many elected officials remained supportive of the administration's policy, mostly because they did not want to be seen as unpatriotic or soft on communism. However, the growing list of American casualties and the high civilian death toll

Watts America Becomes Violent

In 1965, California highway patrolman Lee W. Minikus pulled over a drunk driver in a black neighborhood near the Watts business district of Los Angeles. The driver, a young black man named Marquette Frye, resisted arrest. When the police subdued him a crowd of onlookers became hostile.

Tensions rapidly escalated. Passing white motorists were pulled from their cars and beaten. Stores were looted and burned, and the entire area was plunged into chaos. Irving Bernstein illustrates the scope of the riot in *Guns or Butter:*

> After six days of rioting, the inventory of damage to life and property was immense. The entire south central riot area covered 46.5 square miles of Los Angeles County. . . . No one knew how many rioted and estimates ranged from 10,000 to 80,000. . . . The heaviest damage was along major arteries, where stores were burned, smashed, and looted. The casualties were 34 killed and 1,032 injured.
>
> Watts was hardly the first of the ghetto riots. . . . But Watts differed . . . in many ways: it was much bigger by any standard of measurement, far more broadly publicized, and more significant by an even wider margin. . . . Watts was a national event . . . in fact, it left its mark on the world.

Watts became symbolic of the extreme anger that was boiling over across America, and it marked a critical turning point for the nation. After Watts, social unrest became more widespread and more violent.

Armed National Guardsmen march along a street in Watts as storefronts burn during the 1965 riots.

from the massive bombing campaigns in North Vietnam became too disturbing to ignore. As demonstrations sprouted in the nation's capital and in major cities across the country, more members of Congress were willing to voice opposition. Congressman Jim Scheur observed "widened unrest among the Congressmen about the situation in Vietnam."[61]

Westmoreland implied in speeches he gave in New York City that the voices of dissent at home gave the enemy hope that they could achieve their goal of taking over South Vietnam by simply prolonging the war. Senator George McGovern of South Dakota responded to this charge. "In trying to imply that it is American dissent which is causing the Vietnamese to continue the war, the administration is only confessing the weakness of its own case by trying to silence its critics and confuse the American people."[62]

McGovern and longtime Senate stalwarts like J. William Fulbright and Richard Russell joined Senator Wayne Morse of Oregon and Senate majority leader Mike Mansfield of Montana in opposing the war. Morse had been an opponent of America's involvement in Vietnam since the beginning, providing one of the only two congressional votes in opposition to the Gulf of Tonkin Resolution.

Fulbright and Russell's departure from the prowar lobby was a significant blow to Johnson's congressional base of support, both politically and personally, as they had been his mentors when he was in the Senate, and Fulbright had cosponsored the Gulf of Tonkin Resolution. Lady Bird Johnson described her husband in August 1967 as "way down and grieved, emotionally wearied by the troubles . . . the growing virus of the riots, the rising list of Vietnam casualties, criticism from your own friends, or former friends, in Congress—and most of the complaining is coming from the Democrats."[63]

The Television War

Congress and the public's growing lack of confidence in the administration's handling of the war were magnified by the media's coverage of events in Vietnam and the antiwar movement in America. Vietnam was the first war extensively covered by television, and nightly reports from the front lines brought the pain and trauma of the conflict into people's living rooms. Scores of horrifying images that would become ingrained in the collective American memory found their way over the airwaves: the piles of civilian bodies from the My Lai massacre; a naked girl running in terror from her village, which had been accidentally napalmed by U.S. bombers, the execution of a VC prisoner by Saigon police chief Nguyen Ngoc Loan, the self-immolation of Thich Quang Duc. These images and many like them did their part to influence Americans' opinions against the war.

Kennedy, Johnson, and Nixon all tried to exercise some control over the media's reporting of the war, but all met with failure. From Kennedy's unsuccessful attempt to have *New York Times* reporter David Halberstam reassigned out of South Vietnam to Nixon's failed injunction against the publication of the Pentagon Papers, the government's en-

A young South Vietnamese girl forced to strip off her flaming clothes and other children flee in terror after a U.S. bomber inadvertently dropped napalm on their village in 1972.

deavors to control the messages sent by the media often ran in the face of the First Amendment's freedom of the press. Rules established to control how correspondents observed combat operations were often circumvented by resourceful reporters who used contacts they had made among the Vietnamese to obtain information.

There were attempts by the South Vietnamese government and the American military command in Saigon to censor stories, but as the war went on, it became harder to hide the harsh realities of the conflict. As veteran war correspondent Peter Arnett notes in *Live from the Battlefield: From Vietnam to Baghdad,* "The high command's grand conspiracy to control the information flow collapsed not only in the war zones but at every cocktail party and dinner gathering. Candid remarks about the war's frustrations found their way into the news analyses and magazine articles of the morning."[64]

When the U.S. government could not control what the media reported, Washington blamed the news organizations for focusing on negative stories. Nixon wrote in *No More Vietnams,* "The Vietnam War started the tradition of 'adversarial journalism' that still poisons our national political climate today."[65] The government attempted to focus the news on the accomplishments being made in the pacification efforts in South Vietnam and the battlefield progress of U.S. forces. However, these stories were contradicted by negative stories that appeared on the evening news and only served to give the appearance that the government was out of touch with the situation in Vietnam.

The television reporters in Vietnam and the respected newspaper columnists in the states maintained that they were fulfilling their responsibility to report events as they saw them. In their view, if the stories appeared to be critical of U.S. policy in Vietnam, it was not because of a negative bias against the government but because those policies did not appear to be working. "We had a duty, an obligation, to make our stories as accurate and realistic as possible," notes Ron Steinman, who was NBC News Saigon bureau chief from April 1966 to July 1968. "And that, I believe, we did."[66]

The Whole World Was Watching

The media's coverage of domestic events during the war also helped shape American opinions. The numerous antiwar demonstrations and the assassinations of King on April 4, 1968, and Robert Kennedy on

June 5, 1968, created a picture of a country in chaos. The 1968 Democratic National Convention in Chicago in the last days of August enhanced that image. Antiwar demonstrators, organized by the National Mobilization Committee, or MOBE, planned to descend on the city to bring its antiwar message to the candidates for the Democratic presidential nomination.

Among the groups that came to Chicago was the Youth International Party, or the Yippies. This group of counterculture pranksters, led by Abbie Hoffman and Jerry Rubin, advocated radical change throughout society. They disregarded street protests, slogans, and speeches in favor of attention-grabbing stunts and comical street theater. In Chicago, they planned to nominate a pig named Pigasus for president. They also claimed that they were going to lace the city's water supply with hallucinogenic drugs and let greased pigs loose in the streets of Chicago. These were baseless claims in the group's usual style, but Chicago mayor Richard Daley was not amused.

Delegates at the 1968 Democratic National Convention carry signs protesting the war. Outside, Chicago police clashed violently with a group of radical activists.

As the boss of what was considered the most powerful Democratic machine in the country, Daley carried a great deal of clout with the national party, and he had no intention of being embarrassed during the convention. He called up all 12,000 of the city's police officers, 6,000 national guardsmen, and 7,500 army personnel to secure the city from the 10,000 demonstrators who gathered in the streets.

The violence that followed was caught on camera and played out before the whole country. While delegates inside the convention hall

Trial of the Chicago Seven

On March 29, 1969, a federal grand jury indicted eight protestors for conspiracy to incite a riot during the 1968 Democratic National Convention in Chicago. The defendants were a veritable who's who of the American antiwar movement, as noted in Tom Wells's *The War Within: America's Battle over Vietnam:*

> Those charged included Dave Dellinger, Rennie Davis, Tom Hayden, Abbie Hoffman, Jerry Rubin, Bobby Seale, John Froines, and Lee Weiner. Most of the career lawyers in the Justice Department considered the indictments groundless or iffy and had advised against them. . . . The "Chicago Eight" (later Seven when Seale's case was separated) became a cause célèbre and rallying point for anti-war activists.

The trial began on September 24 and became a farce that gained national attention, with the defendants engaging in speeches, pranks, and other antics that disrupted the proceedings. On February 20, 1970, Dellinger, Davis, Hayden, Hoffman, and Rubin were found guilty of inciting a riot and sentenced to five years imprisonment and a five-thousand-dollar fine. The court of appeals reversed the conviction on November 11, 1972, on the basis of cultural biases of the jurors and presiding judge Julius Hoffman's antagonistic attitude toward the defense.

Members of the Chicago Eight speak with the press before their trial. The activists were charged with inciting a riot during the 1968 Democratic National Convention.

nominated Vice President Hubert Humphrey as their candidate, police and demonstrators clashed in the streets outside. Hundreds were injured by tear gas, mace, and police truncheons in the ensuing fights.

Polls conducted after the convention showed support for Daley's tactics by two to one, and he proudly defended his actions. "This administration and the people of Chicago would never permit a lawless, violent group of terrorists to menace the lives of millions of people, destroy the purpose of a national political convention, and take over the streets."[67]

The events of the convention, however, worked against Humphrey's campaign, and he had a difficult time establishing his position on Vietnam. He wanted to come out openly against the war, but as Johnson's vice president, he could not do this and still maintain a united front with the administration. At this time Johnson was trying unsuccessfully to get the North Vietnamese to negotiate a settlement, and he did not want his vice president to undercut him. To compound Humphrey's dilemma, Johnson did not even openly endorse him until near the end of the race. The Republicans, who had recently nominated Nixon as their candidate, took political advantage of these troubles with a television advertisement that asked, "How can a party that can't keep order in its own backyard hope to keep order in our fifty states?"[68]

On November 5, 1968, Nixon triumphed over Humphrey by just under five hundred thousand votes to become the thirty-seventh president of the United States and the fourth president embroiled in the conflict in Vietnam.

An Appeal to the Silent Majority

Nixon pledged to end the war and bring peace with honor to the United States, but some actions he took to achieve this goal were less than honorable. During the campaign he worked behind the scenes to manipulate the stalled peace talks in his own favor by sending messages to South Vietnam's president Thieu to continue stalling the negotiations until after the election. The North Vietnamese demanded Thieu's removal from office as one of their conditions for peace, and Johnson was anxious to reach an agreement before he left office. Nixon knew that if an armistice was reached prior to the November election, Humphrey's victory would be assured. Playing off Thieu's concerns that America would abandon him to the mercy of the North Viet-

South Vietnamese president Ngyen Van Thieu (left) and U.S. presidential candidate Richard Nixon (right) conspired to thwart President Johnson's efforts to negotiate peace in Vietnam before the 1968 election.

namese, Nixon reached out to Thieu through Anna Chenault, a well-connected businesswoman with ties to Washington, Saigon, and both the Republican and Democratic parties.

In Chenault and Thieu, Nixon found ready allies. But Diem, South Vietnam's ambassador to the United States, remarked that Thieu "thought that Nixon, through his statements, was stronger than Humphrey; Nixon was known to be a very anticommunist politician."[69] Nixon told Thieu that as president he would "see that Vietnam gets better treatment from me than under the Democrats."[70] Consequently, when Johnson finally agreed on October 31, 1968, to a full, unconditional bombing halt to get the North Vietnamese to sit down at the negotiating table, Thieu opposed it, collapsing Johnson's best effort to date and embarrassing Humphrey on the eve of the election. Johnson learned of Nixon's duplicity through FBI wiretaps on Chenault's phone but could not expose the Republican candidate without letting it be known that he was snooping on him.

Despite the lack of progress in the peace talks in Paris, the first few months of Nixon's term in office brought a brief lull in the antiwar demonstrations as the public waited anxiously to see if he would live up to his promise to end the war. However, when his secret bombing campaign in Cambodia became public, protests flared up again across the country. On October 15, 1969, the Moratorium peace demonstration was organized by antiwar groups in Washington and several other U.S. cities. A similar demonstration on November 15 drew 250,000 protesters to the nation's capital for the largest antiwar rally in U.S. history.

By this time demonstrators were no longer being viewed as hippies and troublemakers. Mainstream Americans began taking part in large rallies that gained widespread media attention and encouraged antiwar members of Congress to become more vocal in their calls to end the war. Nixon, in a televised address to the nation on November 3, outlined the proposed withdrawal of U.S. troops from Southeast Asia and turned to "the great silent majority of my fellow Americans,"[71] asking for support in his efforts to end the war honorably for the country.

Nixon earned widespread approval for the speech, but that approval faded as the war dragged on. He had to find a way to end it favorably for the United States and keep from making the same mistakes as Johnson had in alienating Congress and the public, all while American soldiers continued to die in Vietnam.

Manufacturing
Chapter 5 # Peace with Honor

North Vietnam cannot defeat or humiliate the United States.
Only Americans can do that.
—Richard Nixon, address to the nation,
November 3, 1969

W HEN RICHARD NIXON became president in January 1969, 31,000 American soldiers had already died in Vietnam. Over 540,000 soldiers were still stationed there, and over $80 billion had been spent on the war; yet the North Vietnamese showed no interest in reaching a settlement to the conflict that was acceptable to the United States. Domestic unrest over the war had become rampant, and many formerly staunch supporters of America's involvement had become disillusioned. Like Johnson before him, Nixon did not want to be the first American president to lose a war. Unlike Johnson in 1963, however, Nixon entered office with few options available to prevent American defeat in Vietnam.

Nixon believed his best option was to withdraw American troops while shoring up the South Vietnamese military so that it could defend itself against the incessant North Vietnamese insurgence. The problem with this strategy, as Karnow notes in *Vietnam,* was that Nixon had to withdraw troops "without any guarantee that the South Vietnamese army could improve rapidly enough to compensate for the departing U.S. troops. As the size of the American force shrank, moreover, the United States would inevitably lose leverage in its bargaining with North Vietnam."[72]

The first U.S. troops roll out of Saigon in 1969. President Nixon hoped a strengthened South Vietnamese army could resist North Vietnamese aggression without U.S. military aid.

Nixon's Complicated Plan for Peace

In order to get the North Vietnamese to take part in a negotiated settlement of the war, Nixon set in motion a complicated series of moves that he hoped would allow the United States an honorable exit from Southeast Asia and give the South Vietnamese a chance for survival. With over twenty years on the national political scene as a hard-charging anti-Communist in the Senate and as Eisenhower's vice president, Nixon had developed a reputation as a shrewd and calculating political operator. He was also extremely skilled in international relations, having traveled the world and met with scores of foreign leaders.

Nixon's experience led him to believe that the manner in which America disengaged from Vietnam would affect its standing on the world scene. The United States could not be seen as simply cutting and running, leaving the South to be overrun by the Communists. If this were the case, Nixon maintained that allies around the world would lose respect and no longer trust American resolve. The South had to be given a fighting chance to defend itself, and Nixon was determined to give Thieu as much economic aid and military equipment as was needed.

Hanoi had held to their demand that Thieu be removed as a condition of the negotiations—one of many sticking points in the stalled peace talks that had started in Paris on January 2, 1969. They also called for an immediate and complete withdrawal of U.S. forces from Vietnam, an unconditional end to the bombing, and the creation of a coalition government in Saigon that represented the Communists. Ho's August 25 reply to a July 15 letter from Nixon calling for peace illustrate's their inflexible position: "Our Vietnamese people . . . are determined to fight to the end, without fearing the sacrifices and difficulties in order to defend their country and their sacred national rights. . . . [T]he

 **The My Lai Massacre**

On March 16, 1968, members of Charlie Company, First Battalion, committed one of the worst atrocities in American military history in the village of My Lai, South Vietnam. In *Facing My Lai: Moving Beyond the Massacre,* editor David L. Anderson describes the incident:

> Charlie Company was part of Task Force (TF) Barker. . . . TF Barker's mission was to locate and destroy Vietcong main-force combat units in an area that had long been a political and military stronghold for the enemy.
>
> Shortly before 8:00 A.M., helicopters landed the company outside My Lai. Expecting Vietcong resistance, the first and second platoons entered the village with weapons firing. By noon every living thing in My Lai that the troops could find—men, women, children, and livestock—was dead. The total of Vietnamese civilians killed numbered 504, according to North and South Vietnamese sources. The casualties of Charlie Company were one self-inflicted gunshot wound in the foot.

The massacre was hidden from the public for a year before letters to the army by Vietnam veteran Ron Ridenhour sparked an official investigation. Sixteen military personnel were charged with offenses related to My Lai, resulting in five court-martials and one murder conviction for Second Lieutenant William Calley, commander of the company's First Platoon. Calley's life sentence was reduced and he was later pardoned by President Nixon.

United States must cease the war of aggression and withdraw their troops from South Vietnam, respect the right of the population of the South and of the Vietnamese nation to dispose of themselves without foreign influence."[73]

Nixon counted on his reputation as a rabid anti-Communist to draw Hanoi to the negotiating table. He explained this "madman theory" to White House chief of staff H.R. Haldeman. "We'll just slip the word to them that, for God's sake, you know Nixon is obsessed about Communism. We can't restrain him when he's angry—and he has his hand on the nuclear button.' And Ho Chi Minh himself will be in Paris in two days begging for peace."[74]

Nixon let it be known to the North Vietnamese that he was not afraid to escalate the conflict with more bombing. He entertained possible targets like Hanoi, the port at Haiphong, even the elaborate dike system that irrigated much of the North's farmland and controlled flooding during the heavy monsoon rains. Prior to Nixon few had ever considered such a move, because the destruction of the dike system would have caused flooding throughout much of North Vietnam and led to the starvation, displacement, or death of hundreds of thousands of people.

Nixon also placed a focus on the diplomatic front, hoping to drive a wedge between North Vietnam and its principal supporters, China and the Soviet Union. There were already poor relations between China and Russia stemming from territorial disputes in Manchuria and ideological differences between the two powers. China was also wary of Russia's extended military support of North Vietnam, fearing that its own influence in Southeast Asia would be diminished. China could not match the Russians in their aid because the excesses of Mao's Cultural Revolution left the country economically depleted. Also, North Vietnam resented China's efforts to dictate its actions and had no intention of becoming a satellite state of the Communist power to its north.

The Soviets, like the Americans, were tiring of their commitment in Vietnam. While their level of support was nowhere near that of the United States, they believed the North Vietnamese had reached a stalemate, and they wanted to bring an end to the conflict. Plus, Russia was eager to enter into talks with the United States over trade issues and nuclear arms control, two subjects that were of much greater importance than military support of North Vietnam.

*President Nixon (left) shakes hands with Chinese leader Mao Tse-Tung in
February 1972. The leaders met as part of an effort to improve relations
between the United States and China.*

The Chinese reached out separately to the United States in the hope
of creating an alliance to counterbalance Russia's growing strength
in the East, which was traditionally China's sphere of influence. Nixon,
along with his national security adviser Henry Kissinger, skillfully took
advantage of these developments and secretly opened talks with both
the Chinese and the Soviets, hoping to foster better relations with the
Communist superpowers and get them to convince the North Vietnamese to negotiate. Formal meetings took place in China between
Nixon and Mao during Nixon's visit of February 21, 1972, and in
Moscow with Russian leader Leonid Brezhnev during Nixon's May 22
trip to Russia.

The visits did lead to a normalization of relations between the
United States and China and to a reduction of tensions between the
United States and the Soviets but had little effect on North Vietnam's

standing in the war. The independent nature of the North Vietnamese government precluded its accepting guidance from its larger Communist allies.

The Problems with Vietnamization

Even if Hanoi could be convinced to negotiate with the United States, there were still over 125,000 NVA troops in South Vietnam. Nixon was committed to leaving Vietnam with the South having a solid chance at survival and boosted efforts for Vietnamization, a term which meant the gradual shifting of combat responsibilities to the South Vietnamese. He noted, "If they do not assume the majority of the burden in their own defense, they cannot be saved."[75] A massive aid buildup began, with large amounts of supplies and military equipment being sent to the South so that it could defend itself after America's exit.

The push for Vietnamization required U.S. troop withdrawals to coincide with the buildup of the South's forces in order to maintain a large enough counterbalance to the NVA. On June 8, 1969, Nixon met with Thieu at Midway Island in the Pacific to inform him of America's

South Vietnamese forces leave for the front in 1971. Shifting the responsibility for the war from American to South Vietnamese troops was a process called Vietnamization.

impending withdrawal from South Vietnam. A phased troop withdrawal began soon after, with 115,000 U.S. soldiers pulled out by the end of 1969. Troop levels would be reduced to 334,000 by the end of 1970 and down to 156,000 by the end of 1971. By November 30, 1972, only 16,000 advisers remained, the same level of personnel America had in Vietnam in 1963. As Kissinger notes in *White House Years,* after 1969, "we would be in a race between the decline of our combat capability and the improvement of South Vietnamese forces—a race whose outcome was at best uncertain."[76]

The unilateral withdrawal of U.S. troops weakened the American bargaining position with the North Vietnamese because it met one of their key demands without asking for anything in return. Nixon was looking to placate his domestic critics with this move, however, and was hoping for a smooth transition from American control of the military situation to South Vietnamese control. As Nixon's second secretary of defense, James Schlesinger, noted later, though, "The strength, resiliency, and steadfastness of the Saigon forces were more highly valued than they should have been."[77]

An example of the relative lack of capability of the South Vietnamese forces was Operation Lam Son 719, which was executed on January 30, 1971. Supported by U.S. air strikes, South Vietnamese forces entered Laos in an attempt to cut the Ho Chi Minh Trail. They reached their early objectives with skill, but when the NVA regrouped, the South's forces were routed and pulled back in a panicked and confused retreat. Such actions had a negative effect on the morale of the South's troops.

Similarly, American forces began suffering severe morale problems. With fewer troops in Vietnam, those still fighting faced the NVA with less support. The draftees, who were less skilled and less motivated to fight, made up a large portion of those left in the country and were more likely to turn to drugs and be insubordinate. Veteran reporter Neil Sheehan noted the morale situation:

[It was an] Army in which men escaped into marijuana and heroin and other men died because their comrades were stoned on these drugs that profited the Chinese traffickers and the Saigon generals. It was an army whose units in the field were on the edge of mutiny, whose soldiers rebelled against the senselessness of their sacrifice by assassinating officers . . . in "accidental" shootings and "fragging" with grenades.[78]

In the United States stories like Sheehan's caused a further erosion of support for the war. While the phased withdrawal was at first interpreted as good news, many were now calling for the troops to be returned home as quickly as possible. Demonstrations against and outrage over Nixon's handling of the war became even more rampant when the bombing of Cambodia became public.

Expanding the War in Order to End It

In Nixon's view, cutting the supply lines of the North Vietnamese was essential to the success of the South's war effort. This required attacks on the Ho Chi Minh Trail, which ran through Cambodia and Laos. Both nations had a history of struggle against the Communists. In Laos the Pathet Lao guerrillas, supported by Hanoi, controlled about half the country, while the neutralist leader Souvanna Phouma was backed by the United States. In Cambodia the situation was more complex. As leader of the country, Prince Norodom Sihanouk attempted to remain neutral between North Vietnam and the United States. He was deposed on March 18, 1970, by General Lon Nol, who sought to remove the Communist influence from the country. He, in turn, was opposed by Pol Pot and his Communist-backed Khmer Rouge guerrillas, who engaged in a bloody power struggle for control of the country.

Nixon hoped that cutting the Ho Chi Minh Trail would disable the Communist insurgencies in Laos and Cambodia as well as South Vietnam. He elected to keep the bombing of Cambodia secret, however, fearing a negative reaction from the American public and from Congress. "My administration was only two months old," Nixon admitted later, "and I wanted to provoke as little outcry as possible at the outset."[79] The operation was so secret, in fact, that Secretary of Defense Melvin Laird and Secretary of State William Rogers did not find out about it until after it was in progress.

The bombing campaign in Cambodia began on March 17, 1969, as a series of operations called Breakfast, Lunch, Snack, Dinner, and Dessert, and known collectively as Operation Menu. Over the course of the next year over one hundred thousand tons of bombs were dropped

The Kent State Shootings

Demonstrations erupted on college campuses across the nation after Nixon announced the April 30, 1970, U.S. incursion into Cambodia. On May 2, at Kent State University in Ohio, student demonstrators burned down the campus ROTC building. On May 4th several of the demonstrators shouted epithets and threw rocks at the National Guardsmen called in to restore order. Without warning, the guardsmen opened fire.

Edward P. Morgan, author of *The 60s Experience: Hard Lessons About Modern America* explains what happened next:

> As recounted by one observer, "Suddenly, after about 30 seconds, the shooting stopped. One girl was lying on the ground, holding her stomach. Her face was white. There were others, lying on the ground. Some moved. Some didn't. The whole area was one of panic." Four students were killed instantly, two of whom were simply walking across the campus to lunch; nine others were injured, one of whom would be paralyzed for life.

Public reactions were mixed. Many sympathized with the students and expressed anger at the Nixon administration. Others pitied the Guardsmen, whom they thought of as scared kids, and some even expressed the belief that the slain students deserved it.

A young woman cries out over the body of a slain student after National Guardsmen opened fire on demonstrators at Kent State in May 1970.

on NVA base camps and along the Trail in Cambodia. On April 30, 1970, South Vietnamese troops invaded the country, backed by the U.S. Air Force. Nixon announced the incursion in a televised address that night. "We take this action not for the purpose of expanding the war into Cambodia, but for the purpose of ending the war in Vietnam and winning the just peace we all desire."[80]

Many did not accept Nixon's explanation, and widespread demonstrations resulted across the country. Congressional opponents openly questioned the legality of the move, but Nixon steadfastly defended his actions. He notes in *No More Vietnams,* "No reasonable interpretation of the Constitution could conclude that the President, as commander in chief, was forbidden from attacking areas occupied by enemy forces and used by them as bases from which to strike at American and allied troops."[81]

Despite Nixon's views on the matter, domestic political pressure forced him to withdraw U.S. forces from Cambodia on June 30. After the Cambodia invasion, Congress became more involved in how the war was conducted. Feeling the pressure from an agitated public, members of the House and Senate began introducing bills that sought to control how Nixon conducted the war.

Congress Steps In

One of the first actions taken by the Senate to rein in America's involvement in the Vietnam conflict was to repeal the Gulf of Tonkin Resolution on June 24, 1970. This act essentially reversed the president's open-ended power to fight the war and led to the cutting of funding for the war by Congress. As more troops came home, U.S. representatives were bolder in their criticism of the war and felt less obligated to vote in favor of funding the military.

On December 22, 1970, an amendment to a defense spending bill sponsored by Senators Frank Church and Sherman Cooper effectively banned American forces from operating in Laos and Cambodia. The Cooper-Church amendment, as it came to be called, was a demonstration of Congress trumping, with its power of the purse, the president's constitutional prerogative as commander of the military. If funding for military operations was denied, there was nothing the president could do otherwise. Nixon, however, resorted to subterfuge to keep the bombing campaigns in Laos and Cambodia operating. Records of

Jeannette Rankin (wearing glasses), the first female member of Congress, and other women protest the war. After the 1970 invasion of Cambodia, Congress sought to end America's involvement in Southeast Asia.

bombing sorties were falsified and tactical air strikes were logged as traveling to different destinations.

Kissinger, who was deep into negotiations with the North Vietnamese by this point, expressed disappointment at Congress's actions. "The pattern was clear. Senate opponents of the war would introduce one amendment after another, forcing the administration into . . . actions to preserve a minimum of flexibility for negotiations. Hanoi could only be encouraged to stall, waiting to harvest the results of our domestic dissent."[82]

Through their actions to limit the president's ability to conduct the war, Congress demonstrated that it was unconcerned for the outcome of the situation in Southeast Asia beyond the end of America's involvement. They continued to cut funding for aid to South Vietnam as the U.S. military presence there diminished. Their attack on the president's ability to conduct the war continued as well with the War Powers Act, which became law over Nixon's veto on November 7, 1973. This act required the president to seek congressional approval for any military action that resulted in sending troops abroad for over sixty days.

Despite these actions, Nixon remained determined to reach an acceptable settlement of the Vietnam War and used all methods available to him to pursue peace with honor.

To the Bitter End

The North Vietnamese continued stonewalling the Paris peace talks. In an attempt to take advantage of the significantly lowered American presence in the South, the NVA launched the Easter Offensive on March 30, 1972. The NVA hoped to repeat the relative success of the 1968 Tet Offensive by delivering a psychological blow to the U.S. and South Vietnamese effort and thereby ruin Nixon's chances for re-

---

 **The Pentagon Papers**

In June 1967 Defense Secretary Robert McNamara commissioned a private study to compile a full and objective history of American involvement in Vietnam. Daniel Ellsberg, a disillusioned but committed Defense and State Department staffer released a copy of the secret documents to the *New York Times,* which began publishing them June 13, 1971.

The Nixon administration sought an injunction to prevent their publication, but the Supreme Court ruled 6-3 in favor of the *Times.* Justice Hugo Black's concurring majority opinion is quoted in *The Pentagon Papers:*

Only a free and unrestrained press can effectively expose deception in government. And paramount among the responsibilities of a free press is the duty to prevent any part of the Government from deceiving the people and sending them off to distant lands to die of foreign fevers and foreign shot and shell. In my view, far from deserving condemnation for their courageous reporting, The *New York Times,* The *Washington Post* and other newspapers should be commended for serving the purpose that the Founding Fathers saw so clearly. In revealing the workings of government that led to the Vietnam war, the newspapers nobly did precisely that which the founders hoped and trusted they would do.

election in November. An army of 125,000 soldiers rolled through the northern provinces of South Vietnam and along the central highlands to the coast. In some areas South Vietnamese soldiers were overrun and fled in panic, while American advisers assumed command of other units that were abandoned by their commanders.

In response, Nixon authorized Operation Linebacker, a massive bombing campaign that destroyed roads, bridges, factories, and oil facilities across North Vietnam. Over 125,000 tons of bombs were dropped during Linebacker, and the Easter Offensive met with a stunning defeat. Having nothing left to offer militarily, the North Vietnamese agreed to move forward with negotiations. Significant progress was made in the ensuing weeks, including Hanoi's allowing Thieu to remain in Saigon, and Kissinger announced on October 26, "We believe that peace is at hand. We believe that an agreement is within sight."[83] Nixon won reelection on November 7 by the largest landslide in U.S. history to date.

Problems developed, however, due to Thieu's anxiety over being abandoned by the United States. He vehemently disagreed with the provision of the agreement that would allow North Vietnamese forces to remain in South Vietnam, believing he would be at the mercy of the North without U.S. assistance. He submitted a list of changes to the proposal, and the North Vietnamese walked away from the negotiations, claiming that the U.S. was deliberately trying to scuttle the agreement.

In response to their action Nixon initiated Linebacker II, commonly known as the Christmas bombing offensive. From December 18 to December 29, American bombers dropped forty thousand tons of bombs over the Hanoi-Haiphong area in a move that was widely criticized by Nixon's opponents. It did have the effect of bringing North Vietnam back to the negotiations, and Thieu also relented on his demands after being threatened by Washington with the termination of military aid.

On January 27, 1973, the Paris Agreement on Ending the War and Restoring Peace in Vietnam was signed by the United States, North Vietnam, South Vietnam, and representatives of the Vietcong. Thieu was in control of over 75 percent of South Vietnam, but the agreement left North Vietnamese Army personnel in place throughout the country. A provisional government led by the Vietcong was set up with

North Vietnamese representative Le Duc Tho (left) shakes hands with security adviser Henry Kissinger after the Paris Peace Agreement was signed in January 1973.

the goal of creating a coalition government in the future. The United States halted all military activity and removed all personnel from the country. Nixon pledged to Thieu that he would use military force to ensure North Vietnam's compliance with the agreement if necessary, but passage of the Case-Church Amendment of June 19 barred any U.S. military activity in Southeast Asia. South Vietnam was on its own.

Of the agreement, Nixon notes in *No More Vietnams,* "It was not our finest hour—but it was our *final* hour."[84] There has been some debate among historians about whether that final hour could have come earlier than it did. Indeed, many of the items that were part of the final agreement had been settled long before the January 1973 signing. Nixon has been faulted for his phased withdrawal strategy in that he senselessly prolonged the ending of the Vietnam War and caused more American deaths than were necessary. Stephen E. Ambrose, in his biography *Nixon: The Triumph of a Politician, 1962–1972,* draws such a conclusion. "Nearly all the names on the left-hand side of the Vietnam Wall in Washington commemorate men who died in action while Richard Nixon was their commander in chief, and they died after he had decided that the war could not be won."[85]

While Nixon can be faulted for dragging on the war, it should be recognized that he inherited a situation created by a series of fatal mistakes made during the Kennedy and Johnson administrations. Faith in the politically unstable South Vietnamese government, inability to adapt to the nature of the conflict, and poor management of the war in Washington all connived to bring about America's defeat in Vietnam before Nixon came onto the scene.

America
After Vietnam

Epilogue

*Psychologists and sociologists may explain some day what
it is about that distant monochromatic land of green
mountains and fields merging with an azure sea, that for
millennia has acted as a magnet for foreigners who sought
glory there and found frustration.*

—Henry Kissinger, *White House Years*

THE GOVERNMENT OF South Vietnam lasted barely two years before the Communists overran Saigon on April 30, 1975. In the desperate final hours, a thousand Americans—support staff and businessmen who had remained in South Vietnam after the U.S. military pulled out—and six thousand South Vietnamese were shuttled out to Yankee Station in helicopters that were later pushed into the sea to make room for the thousands of refugees crowding the aircraft carrier decks. Over the course of the next several years six hundred thousand more Vietnamese would flee the country to escape imprisonment, political reeducation, and the harsh economic conditions that existed in postwar Vietnam.

In Cambodia, under Pol Pot's brutal dictatorship, 2 million people—one quarter of the country's population—would die from starvation, overwork, and murder. Laos, like South Vietnam and Cambodia, also fell to the Communists, and its people endured sustained misery during periods of civil and economic strife.

Vietnam was embroiled in conflict with its neighbors for much of the rest of the 1970s, and it was not until the 1990s, when the nation became an active member of the international community in trade and diplomatic matters, that its poor economic conditions began to improve. The United States formally recognized Vietnam's nationhood and normalized relations on July 11, 1995, and the two nations have since entered into a bilateral trade agreement.

In the Shadow of the Vietnam War

The normalization of relations between the United States and Vietnam was no easy feat to accomplish. For years, many Americans did not want to face the realities of the war and elected to turn inward away from the world and the country's international responsibilities. The

A weeping South Vietnamese man and his family are forced to leave their village in South Vietnam. Once the North Vietnamese overran Saigon in 1975, thousands of refugees left South Vietnam.

U.S. senators that fought in Vietnam, including John Kerry (second from left) and John McCain (far right), attend a 1997 ceremony at the Vietnam Veterans Memorial in Washington, D.C.

needs of many Vietnam veterans were neglected, and every military engagement that loomed before the country was met with anxiety over whether it would turn into "another Vietnam."

After nearly a decade of silence, Vietnam became a topic of conversation in the 1980s as books and films explored the American experience during the war. People grew to be more comfortable with facing the subject of the war, yet it remains a painful experience for those who fought it and for the families of the more than fifty eight thousand Americans who lost their lives in Southeast Asia.

The war has had a continuing impact on the political scene that can still be witnessed in today's headlines. During the 1992 presidential campaign, Democratic candidate Bill Clinton was accused of dodging the draft during the Vietnam War by requesting a deferment to Oxford University in England, where he supposedly took part in antiwar protests. Republican presidential candidate George W. Bush was accused by his opponents in 2000 and 2004 of using family connections to get him into the Texas Air National Guard during the Vietnam conflict, an assignment that kept him stateside during the war. His opponent in 2004, Senator John Kerry, was also scrutinized for his service and conduct during the war. Kerry received three Purple Hearts and other awards for bravery in Vietnam, but drew lasting criticism upon his return when he testified before Congress as a founding member of Vietnam Veterans Against the War.

The impact of the Vietnam War is likely to stay with us for years to come. It has become an enigma in American history—a turning point in the national consciousness when America realized its vulnerabilities and its imperfections. It has affected the way Americans see themselves and their nation, and it has influenced the decisions the country has made in international relations. But one promise remains as true today as when President Kennedy made it on January 20, 1961: "Let every nation know, whether it wishes us well or ill, that we shall pay any price, bear any burden, meet any hardship, support any friend, oppose any foe to assure the survival and success of liberty."[86]

Notes

Introduction: America Inherits a Civil War

1. Quoted in Stanley Karnow, *Vietnam: A History.* New York: Penguin, 1997, p. 119.
2. Quoted in William J. Duiker, *Ho Chi Minh.* New York: Hyperion, 2000, p. 283.
3. Quoted in James R. Arnold, *The First Domino: Eisenhower, the Military, and America's Intervention in Vietnam.* New York: William Morrow, 1991, p. 65.
4. Quoted in Arnold, *The First Domino,* p. 255.

Chapter 1: South Vietnam: An Uncertain Ally

5. Arthur M. Schlesinger Jr., *A Thousand Days: John F. Kennedy in the White House.* New York: Fawcett, 1965, p. 499.
6. James William Gibson, *The Perfect War: Technowar in Vietnam.* Boston: Atlantic Monthly Press, 1986, p. 71.
7. Schlesinger, *A Thousand Days,* p. 497.
8. Quoted in Bernard B. Fall, ed., *Ho Chi Minh on Revolution: Selected Writings, 1920–1966.* New York: Frederick A. Praeger, 1967, p. 356.
9. H.R. McMaster, *Dereliction of Duty: Lyndon Johnson, Robert McNamara, the Joint Chiefs of Staff and the Lies That Led to the Vietnam War.* New York: HarperCollins, 1997, p. 46.
10. Quoted in Robert S. McNamara, with Brian VanDeMark, *In Retrospect: The Tragedy and Lessons of Vietnam.* New York: Random House, 1995, p. 186.
11. Quoted in David M. Barrett, *Uncertain Warriors: Lyndon Johnson and His Vietnam Advisers.* Lawrence: University Press of Kansas, 1993, p. 30.
12. Quoted in Michael Lee Lanning and Dan Cragg, *Inside the VC*

and the NVA: The Real Story of North Vietnam's Armed Forces. New York: Fawcett Columbine, 1992, p. 34.

13. Quoted in Gibson, The Perfect War, p. 84.
14. Quoted in Karnow, Vietnam, p. 394.
15. Townsend Hoopes, The Limits of Intervention. New York: David McKay, 1969, p. 68.
16. Quoted in Neil Sheehan, Hedrick Smith, E.W. Kenworthy, and Fox Butterfield, The Pentagon Papers: The Secret History of the Vietnam War as Published by the New York Times. New York: Bantam, 1971, p. 141.
17. Quoted in Barbara W. Tuchman, The March of Folly. New York: Alfred A. Knopf, 1984, p. 299.
18. Quoted in Schlesinger, A Thousand Days, p. 905.
19. Karnow, Vietnam, p. 451.

Chapter 2: A New Kind of War

20. Richard Nixon, No More Vietnams. New York: Arbor House, 1985, p. 45.
21. Duiker, Ho Chi Minh, p. 11.
22. Quoted in Barrett, Uncertain Warriors, p. 27.
23. Lanning and Cragg, Inside the VC and the NVA, p. 173.
24. Quoted in Fall, Ho Chi Minh on Revolution, p. 355.
25. Quoted in Arnold, The First Domino, p. 161.
26. Quoted in McMaster, Dereliction of Duty, p. 10.
27. McMaster, Dereliction of Duty, p. 62.
28. Quoted in Irving Bernstein, Guns or Butter: The Presidency of Lyndon Johnson. New York: Oxford University Press, 1996, p. 347.
29. Quoted in Wilbur H. Morrison, The Elephant and the Tiger: The Full Story of the Vietnam War. New York: Hippocrene, 1990, p. 123.
30. Quoted in McMaster, Dereliction of Duty, p. 73.
31. Quoted in McMaster, Dereliction of Duty, p. 233.
32. Quoted in Fall, Ho Chi Minh on Revolution, p. 366.
33. Hoopes, The Limits of Intervention, p. 79.
34. Quoted in Bernstein, Guns or Butter, p. 346.
35. Quoted in Gibson, The Perfect War, p. 348.
36. Quoted in Gibson, The Perfect War, p. 120.

Chapter 3: A Disillusioned Leadership

37. Quoted in Tuchman, The March of Folly, p. 311.

38. Quoted in Karnow, *Vietnam,* p. 339.
39. Quoted in Lloyd C. Gardner, *Pay Any Price: Lyndon Johnson and the Wars for Vietnam.* Chicago: Ivan R. Dee, 1995, p. 90.
40. Quoted in Stephen E. Ambrose, *Nixon: The Triumph of a Politician, 1962–1972.* New York: Simon and Schuster, 1989, p. 54.
41. Quoted in Tuchman, *The March of Folly,* p. 314.
42. Quoted in Sheehan, Smith, Kenworthy, and Butterfield, *The Pentagon Papers,* p. 235.
43. Quoted in Bernstein, *Guns or Butter,* p. 336.
44. Quoted in Barrett, *Uncertain Warriors,* p. 31.
45. Quoted in Karnow, *Vietnam,* p. 421.
46. Quoted in McMaster, *Dereliction of Duty,* p. 88.
47. Quoted in Barrett, *Uncertain Warriors,* p. 39.
48. Quoted in Sheehan, Smith, Kenworthy, and Butterfield, *The Pentagon Papers,* pp. 542–43.
49. Quoted in Marvin E. Gettleman, Jane Franklin, Marilyn B. Young, and H. Bruce Franklin, eds., *Vietnam and America.* New York: Grove, 1995.
50. Quoted in Bernstein, *Guns or Butter,* p. 476.
51. Quoted in Karnow, *Vietnam,* p. 337.
52. McNamara, *In Retrospect,* p. 313.
53. Quoted in Lady Bird Johnson, *A White House Diary.* New York: Holt, Rinehart and Winston, 1970, p. 643.
54. Lyndon Baines Johnson, *The Vantage Point: Perspectives of the Presidency, 1963–1969.* New York: Holt, Rinehart, and Winston, 1971, p. 435.

Chapter 4: The War at Home

55. Quoted in Edward P. Morgan, *The 60s Experience: Hard Lessons About Modern America.* Philadelphia: Temple University Press, 1991, p. 144.
56. Quoted in Bernstein, *Guns or Butter,* p. 380.
57. Quoted in Barrett, *Uncertain Warriors,* p. 81.
58. Quoted in Lady Bird Johnson, *A White House Diary,* p. 555.
59. Quoted in Maurice Isserman and Michael Kazin, *America Divided: The Civil War of the 1960s.* New York: Oxford University Press, 2000, p. 173.
60. Quoted in Tom Wells, *The War Within: America's Battle over Vietnam.* Berkeley and Los Angeles: University of California Press, 1994, p. 299.

61. Quoted in Bernstein, *Guns or Butter,* p. 399.
62. Quoted in Morgan, *The 60s Experience,* p. 140.
63. Quoted in Jeffrey Kimball, *Nixon's Vietnam War.* Lawrence: University Press of Kansas, 1998, pp. 45–46.
64. Peter Arnett, *Live from the Battlefield: From Vietnam to Baghdad.* New York: Simon and Schuster, 1994, p. 219.
65. Nixon, *No More Vietnams,* p. 162.
66. Ron Steinman, *Inside Television's First War: A Saigon Journal.* Columbia: University of Missouri Press, 2002, p. 251.
67. Quoted in Isserman and Kazin, *America Divided,* p. 234.
68. Quoted in Isserman and Kazin, *America Divided,* p. 235.
69. Quoted in Kimball, *Nixon's Vietnam War,* p. 57.
70. Quoted in Ambrose, *Nixon,* p. 208.
71. Quoted in Gettleman, Franklin, Young, and Franklin, eds., *Vietnam and America,* p. 444.

Chapter 5: Manufacturing Peace with Honor

72. Karnow, *Vietnam,* p. 641.
73. Quoted in Henry Kissinger, *White House Years.* New York: Little, Brown, 1979, p. 283.
74. Quoted in Ambrose, *Nixon,* p. 224.
75. Quoted in Ambrose, *Nixon,* p. 146.
76. Kissinger, *White House Years,* p. 272.
77. Quoted in Douglas Kinnard, *The War Managers.* Hanover, NH: University Press of New England, 1977, p. 4.
78. Quoted in Morgan, *The 60s Experience,* pp. 161–62.
79. Quoted in Kimball, *Nixon's Vietnam War,* p. 133.
80. Quoted in Gettleman, Franklin, Young, and Franklin, eds., *Vietnam and America,* p. 454.
81. Nixon, *No More Vietnams,* p. 110.
82. Quoted in Kimball, *Nixon's Vietnam War,* p. 221.
83. Kissinger, *White House Years,* p. 1399.
84. Nixon, *No More Vietnams,* p. 170.
85. Ambrose, *Nixon,* p. 657.

Epilogue: America After Vietnam

86. Quoted in Erik Bruun and Jay Crosby, eds., *Our Nation's Archive: The History of the United States in Documents.* New York: Black Dog and Leventhal, 1999, p. 715.

Chronology

1861
France establishes a colony in what is modern-day Vietnam.

1945
September 2: Ho Chi Minh declares the free and independent Republic of Vietnam. War later breaks out between Ho's Vietminh and the French.

1954
May 7: The Vietminh defeat French forces at Dien Bien Phu. The French relinquish their power in Indochina.

July 21: The Geneva Accord splits Vietnam into the Communist-held North and the non-Communist South, with elections scheduled to unite the country within two years.

1955
October 23: Ngo Dinh Diem becomes president of South Vietnam in a rigged election.

1956–1960
Diem rejects elections to unite the two Vietnams; the United States gives South Vietnam over $2 billion in aid; thousands of Vietcong infiltrators slip into South Vietnam, preparing for an extended guerrilla campaign.

1961
November 1: General Maxwell Taylor advises U.S. president John Kennedy to send troops to Vietnam but warns that reinforcement with larger divisions will be likely.

1963
January 3: South Vietnamese forces are defeated by a smaller Vietcong force at Ap Bac.

May: Buddhist riots in South Vietnam protest Diem's policies.

November 2: Diem is killed after a coup overthrows his government; it is the first of a series of coups that will plague the unstable South Vietnamese government over the next three years.

November 22: Kennedy is assassinated in Dallas; Lyndon Johnson becomes president; Johnson pledges to defend South Vietnam against communism; by year's end over sixteen thousand U.S. military advisers are in Vietnam.

1964

July 1: General William Westmoreland is appointed commander of U.S. forces in Vietnam; he calls for a substantial military buildup in order to wipe out the Vietcong presence in the South.

August 2: USS *Maddox* is attacked by North Vietnamese patrol boats in the Gulf of Tonkin; Johnson orders no action in response.

August 3: Another attack in the Gulf of Tonkin, which may not have taken place, prompts a measured response from U.S. bombers.

August 7: Congress passes the Gulf of Tonkin Resolution, giving Johnson wide authority to prosecute a war against North Vietnam.

November 3: Johnson is reelected by the largest landslide in American history; by year's end twenty-three thousand U.S. soldiers are in Vietnam.

1965

A massive buildup of U.S. military personnel and construction takes place in South Vietnam; the first of what will become widespread antiwar demonstrations begin on college campuses around the country.

March 2: Operation Rolling Thunder, a bombing campaign, begins; it will last for three years; by year's end 184,000 U.S. soldiers are in Vietnam.

1966

October 14: Defense Secretary McNamara submits a report to Johnson stating that the bombing of North Vietnam is having no effect on enemy morale or their ability to continue the war.

1967

October 31: Fifty thousand protestors march on the Pentagon.

1968

January 30: The North Vietnamese and Vietcong launch the Tet Offensive, striking over hundred targets across South Vietnam; the effort is defeated in a matter of weeks, but many Americans interpret the attack as sign of a stalemate in Vietnam.

February 29: McNamara resigns as secretary of defense.

March 31: With support at an all-time low, Johnson announces that he will not seek reelection.

August: Demonstrators and police clash at the scene of the Democratic National Convention in Chicago; Vice President Hubert Humphrey wins the nomination.

November 5: Richard Nixon narrowly defeats Humphrey to win the presidency; he pledges to bring peace with honor; by year's end, there are over 540,000 U.S. soldiers in Vietnam.

1969

January 25: Peace talks begin in Paris.

March 17: Nixon begins secret bombing of Cambodia.

June 8: Nixon executes a phased withdrawal of U.S. forces from Vietnam.

October 15: The Moratorium antiwar demonstration draws thousands across the country.

November 3: Nixon appeals to the "great silent majority" of Americans to support his plan to end the war.

November 15: A crowd of 250,000 antiwar protesters converge on Washington, D.C.; by year's end 115,000 U.S. soldiers are removed from Vietnam.

1970

April 30: U.S. and South Vietnamese forces invade Cambodia; massive criticism and demonstrations force U.S. withdrawal on June 30.

June 24: Congress repeals the Gulf of Tonkin Resolution.

December 22: Cooper-Church Amendment bans American military operations in Laos and Cambodia. By year's end 334,000 U.S. soldiers are in Vietnam.

1971

January 30: South Vietnamese forces attack North Vietnamese bases in Laos, in the first largely South Vietnamese military operation; it is hailed a success of Vietnamization, but ends in failure. By year's end 156,000 U.S. soldiers are in Vietnam.

1972

February 21: Nixon travels to Beijing to meet with Chinese leader Mao

Zedong and normalize relations between the United States and China.
March 30: North Vietnamese launch the Easter Offensive across South
Vietnam; it is beaten back by widespread U.S. bombing.
May 22: Nixon travels to Moscow to meet with Soviet leader Leonid
Brezhnev and begin the process of détente with the Soviets.
November 7: Nixon is reelected in the largest landslide in U.S. history.
November 30: Only 16,000 U.S. military advisers remain in Vietnam.

1973
January 27: Paris Agreement on Ending the War and Restoring Peace
in Vietnam ends the war; the last U.S. troops are pulled out of the country.
November 7: Congress passes War Powers Act, requiring the president
to seek congressional approval for any military actions that last longer
than sixty days.

1975
April 30: North Vietnamese forces overrun Saigon and take control
of South Vietnam; the country is united under one Communist government.

1995
July 11: The United States and Vietnam normalize relations.

For Further Reading

Books

American Heritage Illustrated History of the United States. Vol. 17, *The Vietnam Era.* New York: Choice Publishing, 1988. An illustrated history of the Vietnam War and the antiwar movement in the United States.

Gil Dorland, *Legacy of Discord: Voices of the Vietnam War Era.* Dulles, VA: Brassey's, 2001. A collection of interviews with high-profile figures from the Vietnam era and the present day, including Daniel Ellsberg, Alexander Haig, Tom Hayden, John Kerry, John McCain, and Norman Schwarzkopf.

Bernard Edelman, *Dear America: Letters Home from Vietnam.* New York: W.W. Norton, 1985. A poignant collection of letters from soldiers in Vietnam to their families and friends in the States.

Anthony James Joes, *The War for South Vietnam, 1954–1975.* Westport, CT: Praeger, 2001. An inquiry into the conflict in Vietnam that examines the connection between the fall of South Vietnam and the fall of the Soviet empire.

Anita Louise McCormick, *The Vietnam Antiwar Movement in American History.* Berkeley Heights, NJ: Enslow, 2000.

Melvin Small, *Johnson, Nixon, and the Doves.* New Brunswick, NJ: Rutgers University Press, 1989. A look at the evolution of political opposition to the war and how Presidents Johnson and Nixon dealt with it.

Web Sites

United States in Vietnam (www.historyplace.com). This Web site at the History Place provides a comprehensive timeline with quotes and analyses.

The Vietnam War, 1965–1973: America's Longest War (www.vietnamwar.com). An extensive list of information and links to biographies, events, battles, statistics, timelines, and maps are offered at this Web site.

The Vietnam War Index (www.spartacus.schoolnet.co.uk/vietnam.html). Spartacus International provides updated listings of political and military figures and issues and events related to the war.

Works Consulted

Books

Stephen E. Ambrose, *Nixon: The Triumph of a Politician, 1962–1972.* New York: Simon and Schuster, 1989. This second volume of an extensive three-volume biography on Richard Nixon focuses on his reemergence on the national political scene in the 1960s and his first term in office.

David L. Anderson, ed., *Facing My Lai: Moving Beyond the Massacre.* Lawrence: University Press of Kansas, 1998. A collection of essays that examine the social, legal, and military impact of the massacre at My Lai.

Dale Andradé, *Ashes to Ashes: The Phoenix Program and the Vietnam War.* Lexington, MA: Lexington Books, 1990. An examination of the clandestine work of the CIA during the Vietnam War, focusing on the Phoenix Program as an element of American military policy.

Peter Arnett, *Live from the Battlefield: From Vietnam to Baghdad.* New York: Simon and Schuster, 1994. This firsthand account of a combat war correspondent in Vietnam illustrates the dangers of the job and the battles fought with government bureaucracy over the reporting of events.

James R. Arnold, *The First Domino: Eisenhower, the Military, and America's Intervention in Vietnam.* New York: William Morrow, 1991. A thorough analysis of the decisions and actions that dictated America's policy toward Vietnam during the 1950s.

David M. Barrett, *Uncertain Warriors: Lyndon Johnson and His Vietnam Advisers.* Lawrence: University Press of Kansas, 1993. An examination of the debates that raged within the Johnson administration over the escalation of America's involvement in Vietnam.

Irving Bernstein, *Guns or Butter: The Presidency of Lyndon Johnson.* New York: Oxford University Press, 1996. A review of Johnson's presidency, including its early policy successes and its ultimate failure in the quagmire of Vietnam.

Erik Bruun and Jay Crosby, eds., *Our Nation's Archive: The History of the United States in Documents.* New York: Black Dog and Leventhal, 1999. Extensive reference collection of important American documents from colonial times to the impeachment acquittal of President William Jefferson Clinton.

William J. Duiker, *Ho Chi Minh.* New York: Hyperion, 2000. Extensive biography of the North Vietnamese leader and the inspiration for his actions.

Bernard B. Fall, ed., *Ho Chi Minh on Revolution: Selected Writings, 1920–1966.* New York: Frederick A. Praeger, 1967. A collection of Ho's essays, speeches, and interviews that provide insight into his beliefs and policies.

Lloyd C. Gardner, *Pay Any Price: Lyndon Johnson and the Wars for Vietnam.* Chicago: Ivan R. Dee, 1995. Relying heavily on documents from the Johnson Presidential Library, this work examines the diplomatic and political miscalculations that led to failure in Vietnam.

Marvin E. Gettleman, Jane Franklin, Marilyn B. Young, and H. Bruce Franklin, eds., *Vietnam and America.* New York: Grove, 1995. A comprehensive collection of documents, speeches, and writings pertaining to many aspects of the Vietnam War.

James William Gibson, *The Perfect War: Technowar in Vietnam.* Boston: Atlantic Monthly Press, 1986. An examination of the strategy the United States developed in fighting the war.

Townsend Hoopes, *The Limits of Intervention.* New York: David McKay, 1969. This account of the failure of U.S. policy in Vietnam was written by a Pentagon staffer and former undersecretary of the air force.

Maurice Isserman and Michael Kazin, *America Divided: The Civil War of the 1960s.* New York: Oxford University Press, 2000. A look at the turbulent decade and how the war and social issues strained American society.

Lady Bird Johnson, *A White House Diary.* New York: Holt, Rinehart, and Winston, 1970. The published diary of the First Lady, covering 1963 to 1969, when her husband, Lyndon Johnson, was in office.

Lyndon Baines Johnson, *The Vantage Point: Perspectives of the Presidency, 1963–1969.* New York: Holt, Rinehart, and Winston, 1971. An extensive autobiographical account of Johnson's time in office that attempts to explain the reasoning behind his actions as president.

Stanley Karnow, *Vietnam: A History.* New York: Penguin, 1997. This authoritative account delves deeply into the history of the Vietnamese people and provides extensive coverage of the war.

Jeffrey Kimball, *Nixon's Vietnam War.* Lawrence: University Press of Kansas, 1998. This book, which focuses exclusively on Nixon's policies regarding Vietnam, is based on research from declassified government documents.

Douglas Kinnard, *The War Managers.* Hanover, NH: University Press of New England, 1977. This analysis of the views of America's commanders during the Vietnam War is drawn from surveys and extensive interviews conducted by the author.

Henry Kissinger, *White House Years.* New York: Little, Brown, 1979. Extensive autobiographical account of Kissinger's time in the White House as national security adviser for Richard Nixon.

Michael Lee Lanning and Dan Cragg, *Inside the VC and the NVA: The Real Story of North Vietnam's Armed Forces.* New York: Fawcett Columbine, 1992. This book reveals the methods of recruiting, training, and commanding the forces of the North Vietnamese during the war.

H.R. McMaster, *Dereliction of Duty: Lyndon Johnson, Robert McNamara, the Joint Chiefs of Staff and the Lies That Led to the Vietnam War.* New York: HarperCollins, 1997. A frank accounting of the subterfuge that existed among the civil and military policy makers during the prosecution of the Vietnam War.

Robert S. McNamara, with Brian VanDeMark, *In Retrospect: The Tragedy and Lessons of Vietnam.* New York: Random House, 1995. A critical review of the decisions and actions that led to failure in Vietnam by one of the men who was principally responsible for America's involvement in that war.

Edward P. Morgan, *The 60s Experience: Hard Lessons About Modern America.* Philadelphia: Temple University Press, 1991. An exploration of the antiwar and civil rights movements through first-person material and narrative accounts.

Wilbur H. Morrison, *The Elephant and the Tiger: The Full Story of the Vietnam War.* New York: Hippocrene, 1990. A step-by-step account of the war that illustrates how the military advantage of the United States was undermined by policy in Washington.

Richard Nixon, *No More Vietnams.* New York: Arbor House, 1985. The former president responds to criticisms against the U.S. government in its prosecution of the war in this biased but insightful book.

Douglas Pike, *Vietcong: The Organization and Techniques of the National Liberation Front of South Vietnam.* Cambridge, MA: MIT Press, 1966. An analysis of the methods the National Liberation Front employed in their efforts to overthrow the South Vietnamese government.

Arthur M. Schlesinger Jr., *A Thousand Days: John F. Kennedy in the White House.* New York: Fawcett, 1965. This Pulitzer prize–winning book by one of John Kennedy's special assistants is considered an authoritative resource on the Kennedy presidency.

Neil Sheehan, Hedrick Smith, E.W. Kenworthy, and Fox Butterfield, *The Pentagon Papers: The Secret History of the Vietnam War as Published by the* New York Times. New York: Bantam, 1971. This analysis of the classified Pentagon research study on America's involvement in Vietnam through 1968 includes key government documents.

Ron Steinman, Inside Television's First War: A Saigon Journal. Columbia: University of Missouri Press, 2002. An autobiographical account from the Saigon bureau chief of NBC News during the Vietnam War.

Maxwell D. Taylor, *Swords and Plowshares.* New York: W.W. Norton, 1972. Autobiography of the chairman of the Joint Chiefs of Staff, 1962–1964, and American ambassador to South Vietnam, 1964–1965.

Barbara W. Tuchman, *The March of Folly.* New York: Alfred A. Knopf, 1984. A fascinating exploration of the role human nature has played in some of history's monumentally bad decisions, from the Trojan War to the Vietnam War.

Douglas Valentine, *The Phoenix Program.* New York: William Morrow, 1990. An in-depth look at the once-secret counterterrorism program conducted by the CIA during the Vietnam War.

Tom Wells, *The War Within: America's Battle over Vietnam.* Berkeley and Los Angeles: University of California Press, 1994. A history of the turmoil in America during the war, with a particular focus on the antiwar movement.

Index

Picture Credits

About the Author

This is Richard Brownell's second title for Lucent's History's Great Defeats Series. His first, *The Fall of the Confederacy and the End of Slavery,* was published in 2005. He has written two stage plays that have received numerous productions around the country and also writes political commentary for various periodicals and Internet sites. He holds a Bachelor of Fine Arts degree from New York University, where he was also recognized for Senior Achievement in Screenwriting. Richard lives in New York City.